Hiking Northwest Montana

All maps used in this book are courtesy of the USGS/U.S. Forest Service and were produced using the online map viewer CalTopo. Visit caltopo.com for more information. All hike GPS files were recorded by the author.

Hiking is a great way to enjoy the outdoors. But first, make sure you are prepared appropriately before hitting the trails. The author assumes no liability for accidents happening to or injuries sustained by readers who engage in the activities described in this book.

ISBN: 979-8-218-01755-2

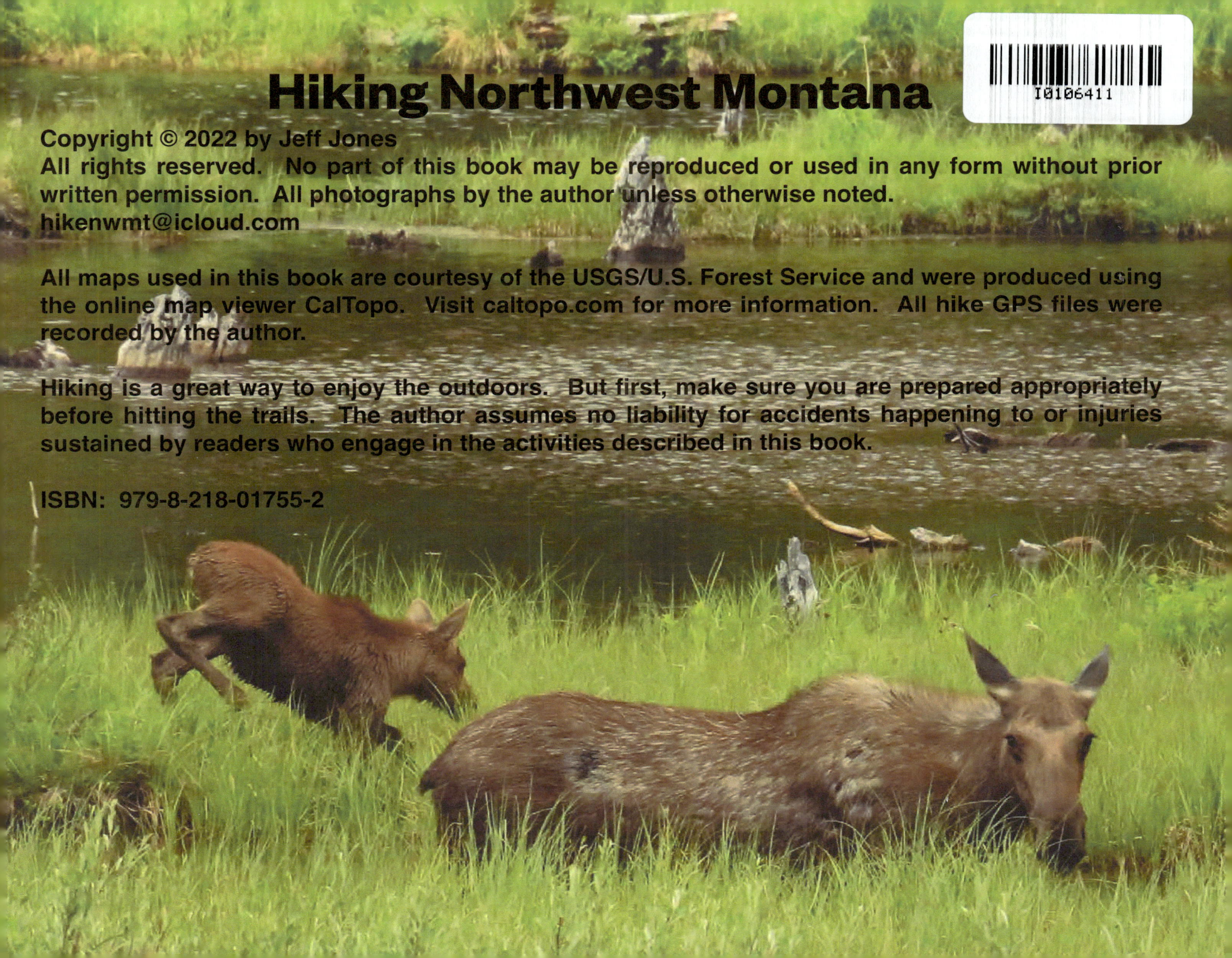

Table of Contents

Glacier National Park

Table of Contents Continued

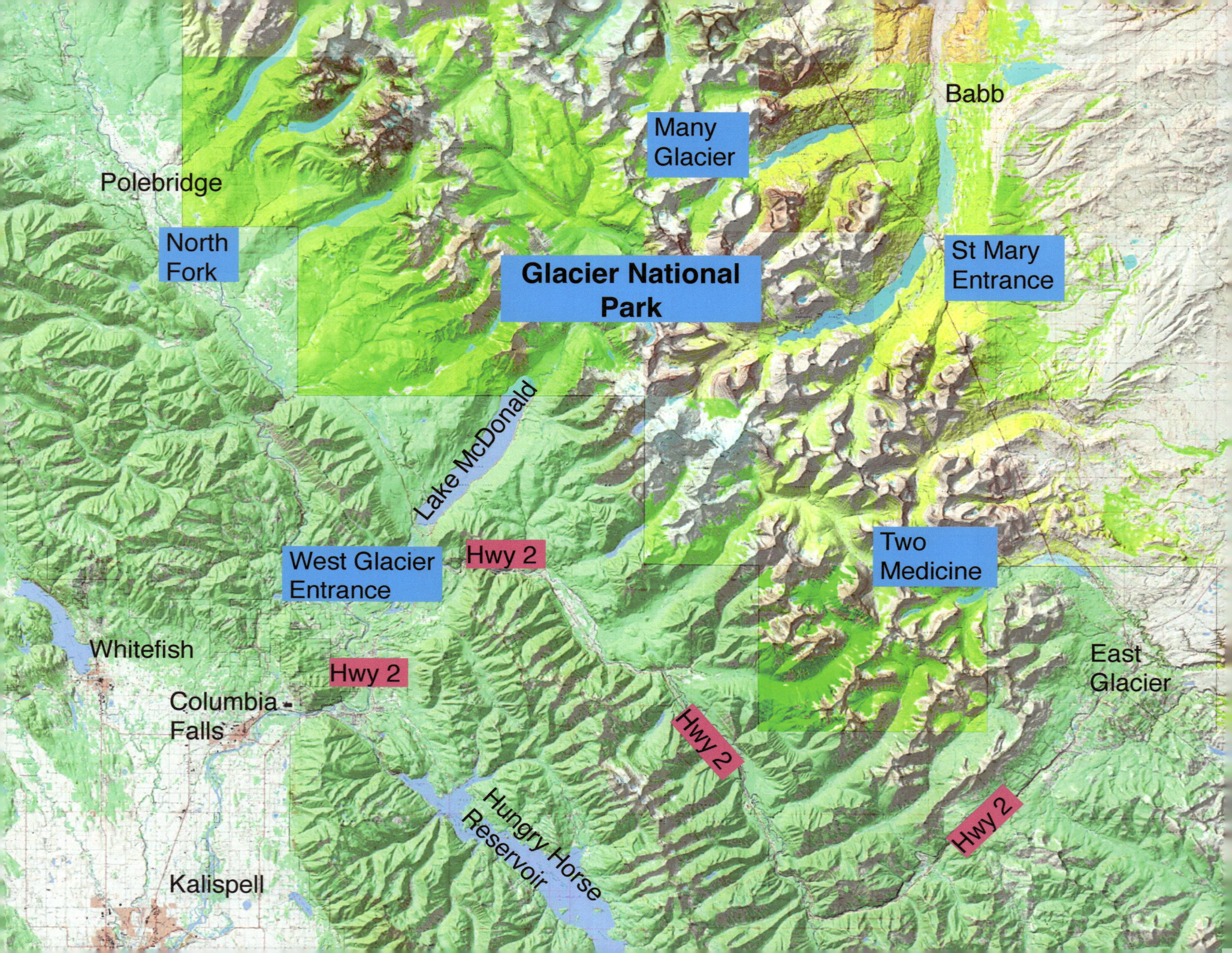

Babb

Many
Glacier

Polebridge

North
Fork

St Mary
Entrance

**Glacier National
Park**

Lake McDonald

West Glacier
Entrance

Hwy 2

Two
Medicine

Whitefish

Hwy 2

East
Glacier

Columbia
Falls

Hwy 2

Kalispell

Hungry Horse
Reservoir

Hwy 2

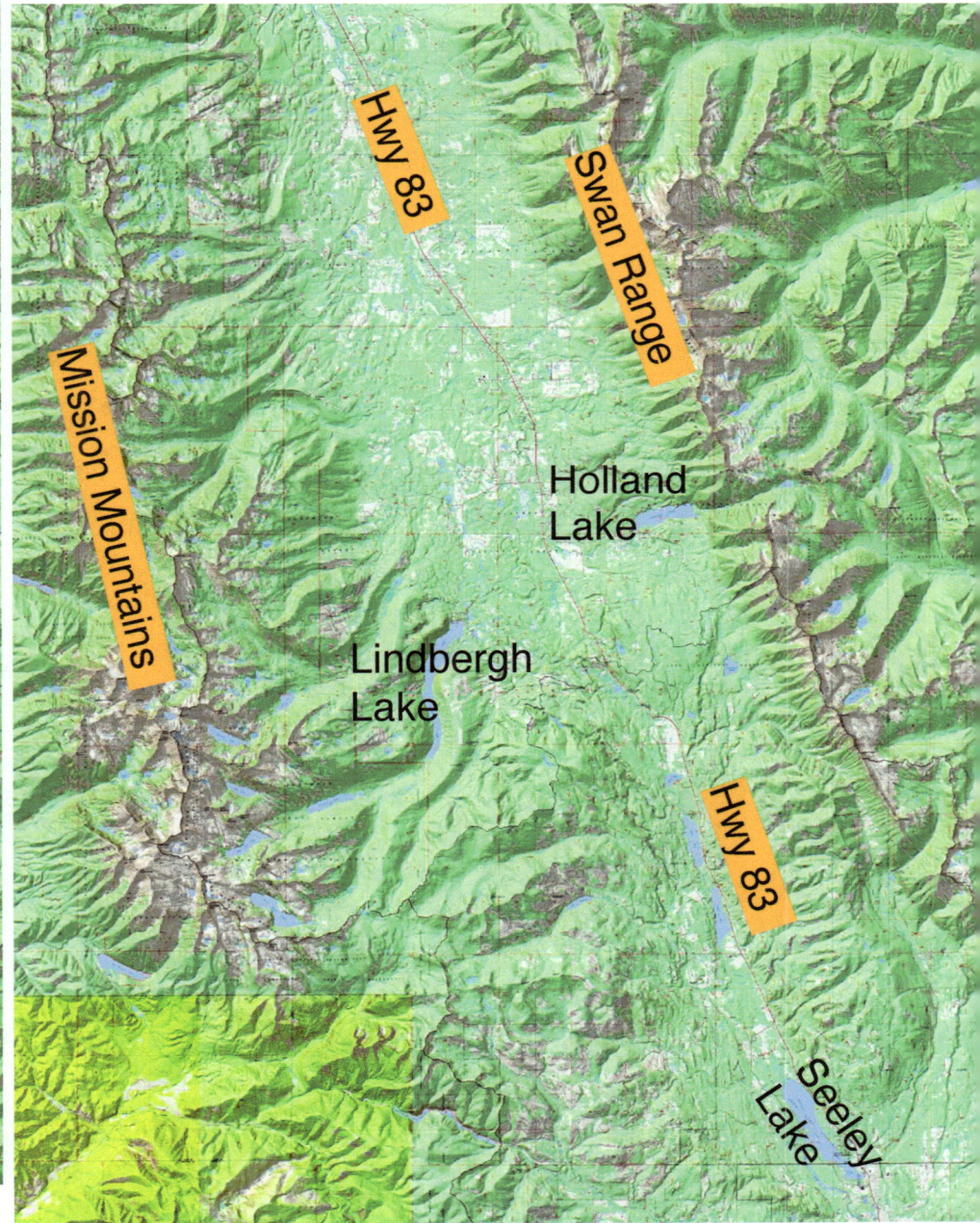

Hwy 83 North

Jewel Basin

Bigfork

Hwy 83

Hungry Horse Reservoir

Swan Lake

Swan Range

Flathead Lake

Hwy 83

Mission Mountains

Hwy 83 South

Hwy 83

Swan Range

Mission Mountains

Holland Lake

Lindbergh Lake

Hwy 83

Seeley Lake

Introduction

Hello hikers and welcome to my guide! Good news…you are in a great place. Northwest Montana is a hikers paradise and has plenty of trails and hiking opportunities.

I started this guide as an aid to help with the hike selection process. Pondering over maps and information while planning a hike, I was frequently left asking which hike to do. When you have your hiking shoes on, I hope this guide can help you pick a rewarding hike with some great views too!

Using this hiking guide

Each hike provides details including GPS (Global Positioning System) profiles and some scenery highlights you'll find. The GPS elevation changes and distances recorded are approximate, but in my view fairly accurate and provide a good hike summary regarding distance, overall time, and elevation change to help you plan. The time recorded is overall and includes breaks and for me plenty of time monkeying around with my camera and taking photos. So your hiking time may vary.

This guide does not rate the hikes as easy or difficult. Everyone is different and in their own specific conditioning. What people pack varies too and can factor, for instance above normal gear and nutrition I typically stuff in an additional 10 pounds of camera gear. To assist individual hikers determine the level of difficulty for them, I include profiles for each hike. I do provide some comments about the trails that may prove helpful in planning and selecting a hike.

All of hikes included in this guide were completed as day hikes. Some trails and lakes allow overnight camping and some do not. Check with the forest service or park rangers and plan accordingly before pitching your tent.

The chapters and sections group hikes in common regions or access points, but there are a few exceptions. I've grouped a number of hikes under "West Glacier Entrance" section since that is my typical entrance into Glacier National Park, but you could also get to these coming from the east side using the Saint Mary Entrance.

Glacier National Park requires reserving car entry tickets. Check with the park and recreation.gov for details and purchasing.

Shuttles operate in Glacier National Park that may be helpful for some hikes. Check with the Park for details and schedule.

Some Abbreviations:

CG - Campground	OB - Out and Back
GNP - Glacier National Park	PTP - Point to Point
LO - Lookout	RT - Round Trip
OL - Overlook	TH - Trailhead

About the author

Jeff Jones is a Montana native and grew up playing outside in Northwestern Montana. He earned a Bachelor of Science degree in Electrical Engineering and worked over 30 years in the high tech industry. He enjoys being outside and exploring, and is also an avid runner and marathoner and has completed marathons on all 7 continents including all World Marathon Majors.

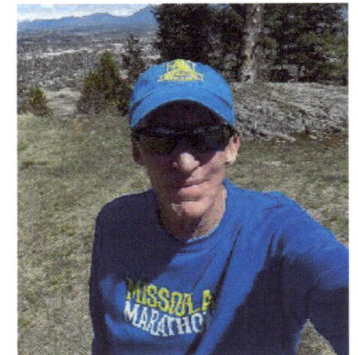

Comments on gear

Weather can change quickly in Northwest Montana so make sure to pack something if it does. I prefer layers like tech running shirts as the base and include a light weight hooded gore tex jacket for outer protection if needed. I throw in a rolled up plastic garage bag that can also help keep things dry or separated, and if you pop holes for arms and neck it can serve as a rain poncho.

- Bear spray (this is bear country). Accessible like on pack waist belt.
- Bear bells so you don't surprise them.
- Bug spray
- Sun block
- Sunglasses
- Camera
- Don't go cheap on the hiking shoes or socks. They keep your feet happy. I prefer lighter, flexible trail running shoes: Hoka One One Speedgoats are great.
- GPS can be handy on the trail.
- Band Aids, first aid.
- Light weight trekking poles. I hike more efficiently and faster especially going up or down hills when using poles.
- Maps and compass. Know your route before hand. Cairn maps out of Missoula Montana are great.
- Having a whistle or aerosol boat horn can be handy if you need to signal or scare something off.
- Hat for sun protection and/or warmth.
- Gloves. Morning starts can be cool and if climbing high it can be cold.
- A good day pack with support, waist belt with pockets, light frame with back ventilation is great. I like 30-36 Liter capacity for medium to long day hikes.
- Appropriate hiking layers and clothing.

- Don't forget to pack plenty of nutrition and drinks to cover distance and time expected on the trail. I like a mix of water and sports drinks.
- Remember to leave no trace. Pack out what you packed in.

Gear

On with the hikes...

**Glacier National Park
West Glacier Entrance**

Ahern Pass from The Loop

Overview: 17.5 mile OB starting at The Loop TH. At about 3.5 miles take a marked left fork towards Granite Park CG and eventually intersect the Highline trail at about 4 miles. Go left on the Highline trail heading north towards Ahern Pass for another 4 miles before reaching the right fork to Ahern Pass.

- Most of the climbing is in the first 4 miles to the Highline trail intersection. Steady grade but not killer steep.
- Trails are in great shape.   Hardly anyone on Highline trail north of Granite Park Chalet 😀!
- Great views along the Highline trail and at Ahern Pass you can see Helen Lake, Lake Elizabeth and Ahern Glacier.
- Parking at The Loop TH can go quick. Start early before sunrise and beat the heat on the first uphill miles.
- If you make reservations and stay at Granite Park Chalet, make it shorter multi day hikes.

Getting to the TH: Continue on Going to the Sun Road past Lake McDonald towards Logan Pass.   Park at The Loop TH at 1st hairpin corner.   Parking can go quick.   TH has bathrooms.

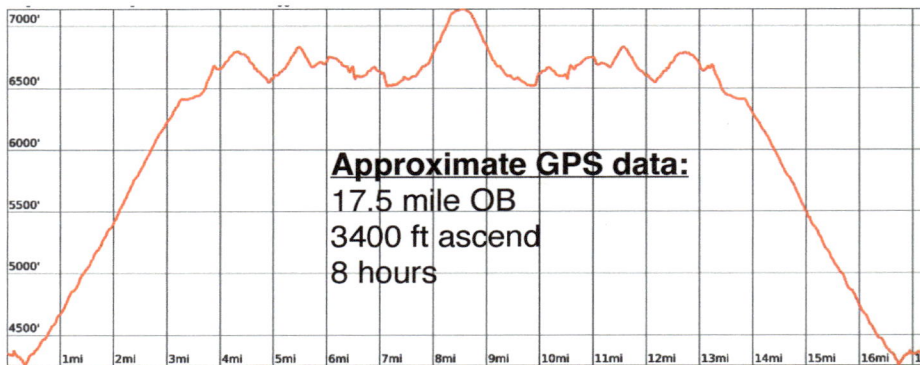

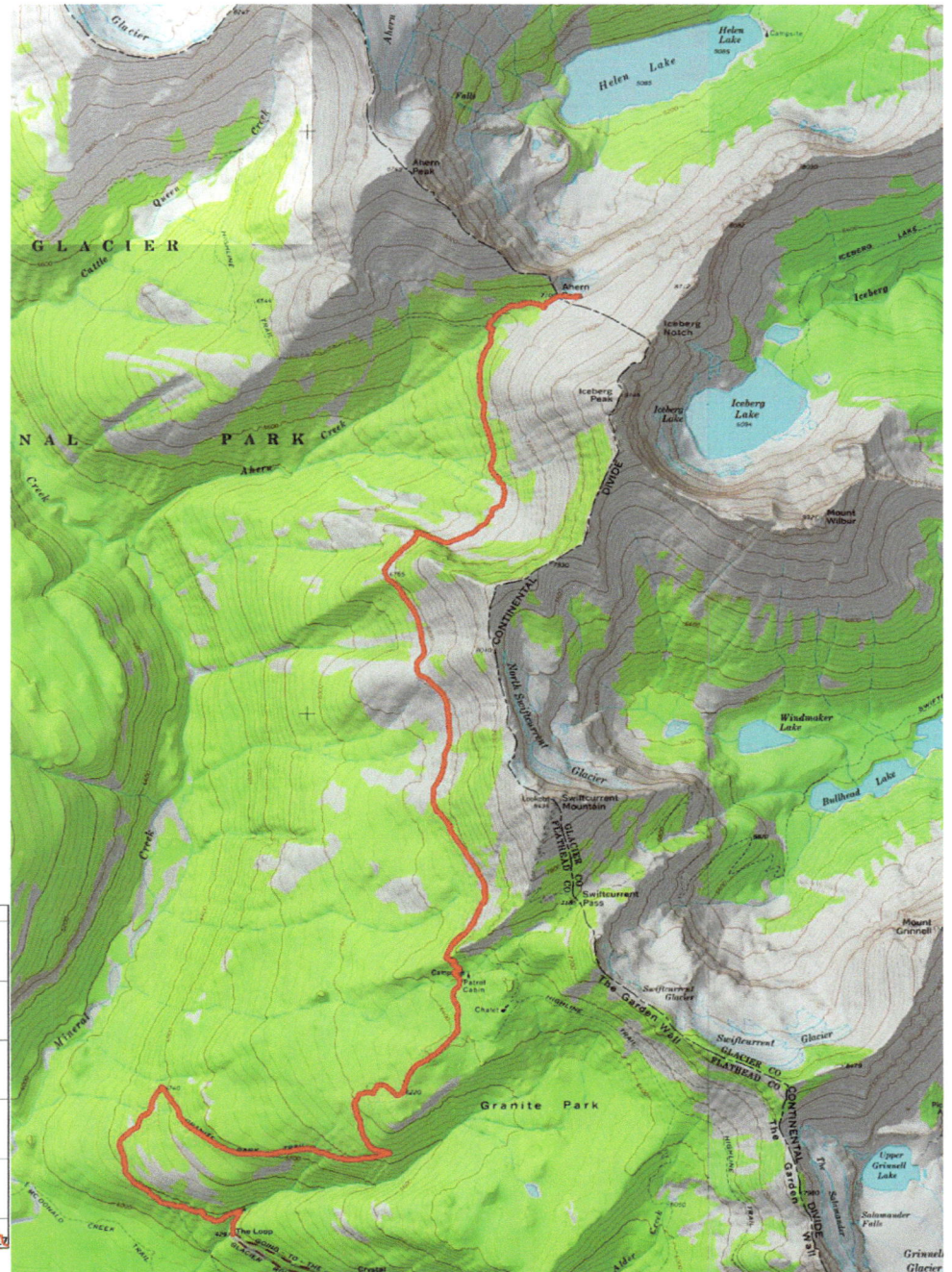

Approximate GPS data:
17.5 mile OB
3400 ft ascend
8 hours

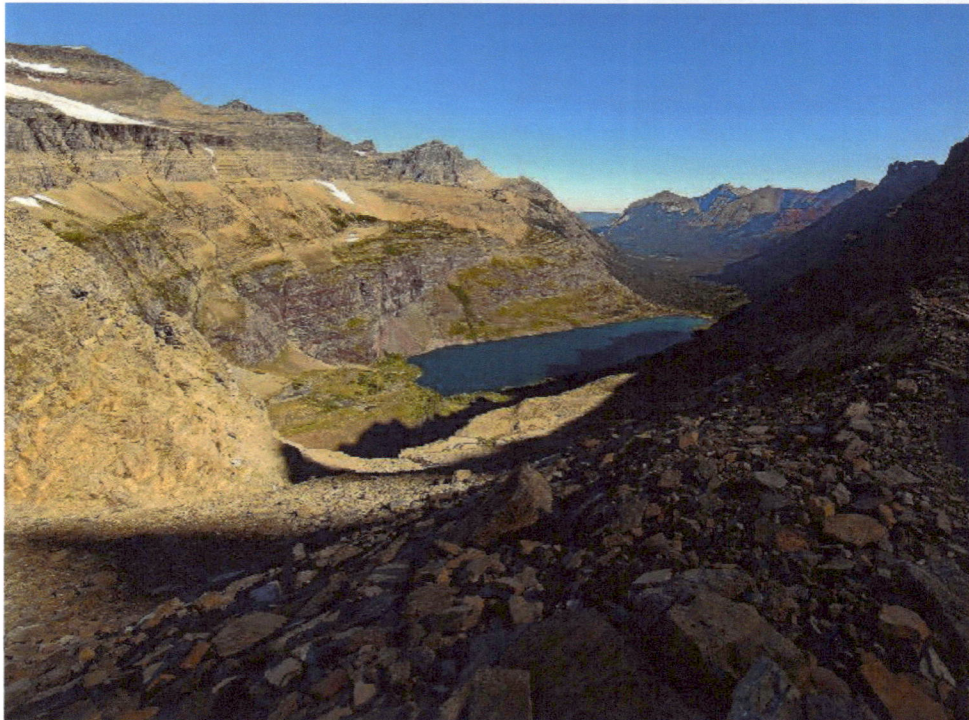

Ahern Pass from The Loop   West Glacier Entrance   Glacier National Park

Apgar Lookout

Overview: 7.2 mile OB.
- Trail in good shape and grade pretty easy.
- Can be buggy especially lower.
- Trail has a lot of sun exposure.
- Plenty of wild flowers June - July.
- Views of Lake McDonald and surrounding mountains.
- Can be a winter hike option. Road likely closed near the horse stables before the bridge that crosses McDonald Creek. The hike adds about 2 miles each way on the road to the TH and is mostly easy rolling grades. Park in plowed lot across from the horse stables.

Getting to the TH: Enter West Glacier and take left towards Glacier Institute before getting to the Apgar Village intersection. After a short distance take a right and soon followed by a left, then proceed almost 2 miles on single lane gravel road to large parking area at TH. There is a bathroom on the way by the horse stables.

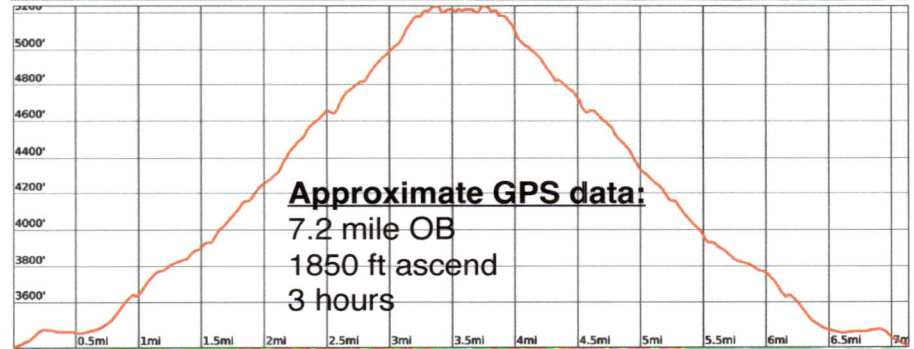

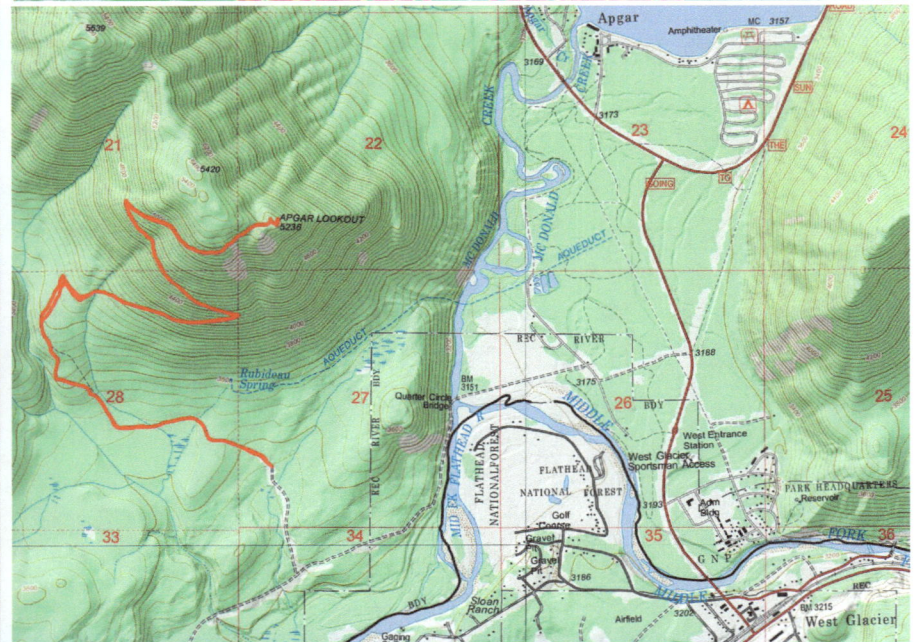

Approximate GPS data:
7.2 mile OB
1850 ft ascend
3 hours

Avalanche Lake & Trail of the Cedars

Overview: 4.7 mile OB to foot of lake and can continue to the head of the lake for 6.5 miles RT. Trail begins on the Trail of the Cedars Nature loop; the Avalanche Lake Trail is marked and branches off this. Scenic Avalanche Creek and Lake. Forest provides plenty of shade. Trail can be quite busy and crowded.

Getting to the TH: Continue past Lake McDonald on Going to the Sun Road to marked TH pullouts on both sides of road. Very popular trail and parking can be scarce. TH has bathrooms.

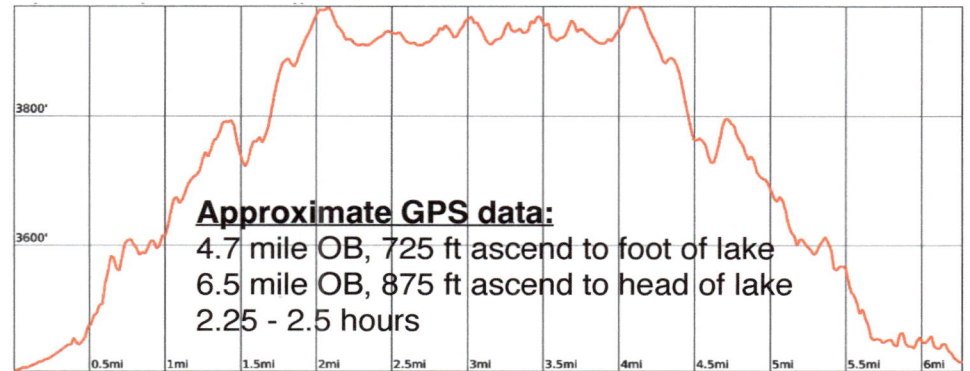

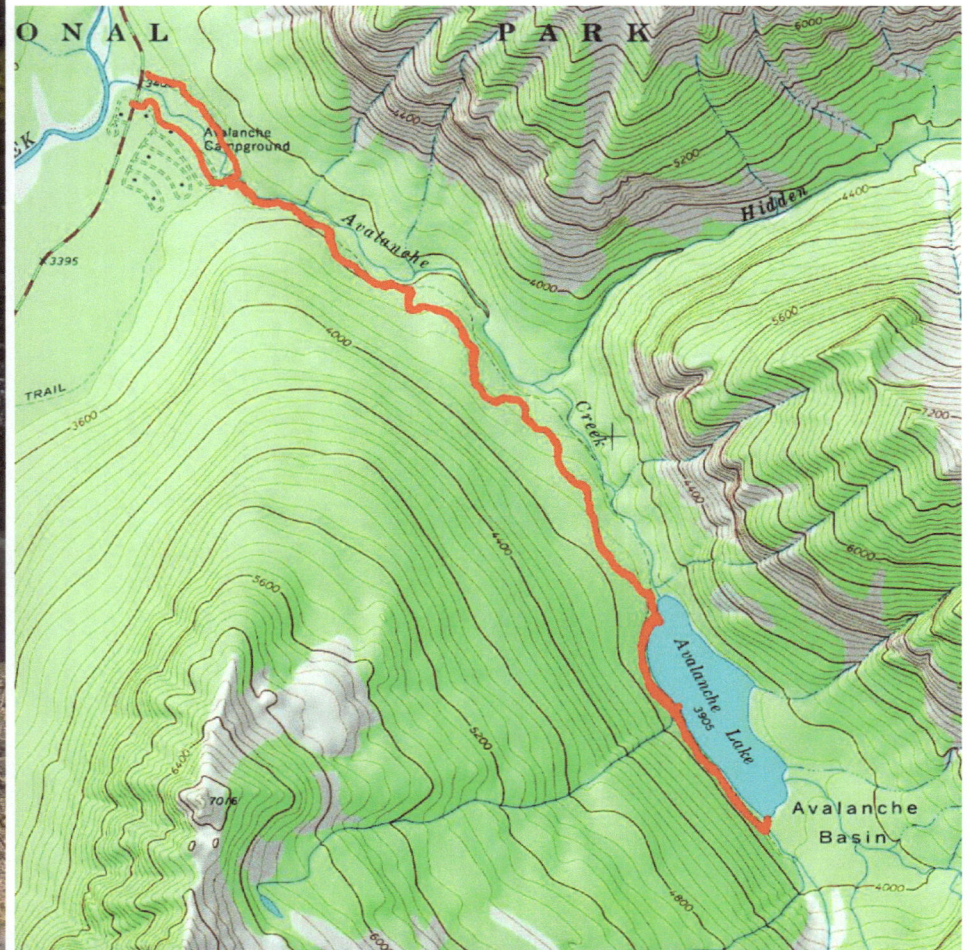

Approximate GPS data:
4.7 mile OB, 725 ft ascend to foot of lake
6.5 mile OB, 875 ft ascend to head of lake
2.25 - 2.5 hours

Avalanche Lake (Winter Edition)

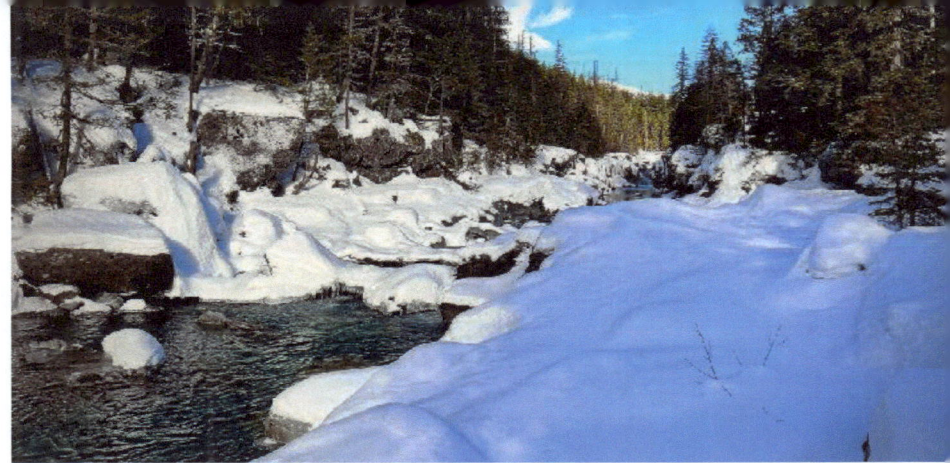

Overview: 16.5 mile OB. In the winter the Going to the Sun Road is closed at Lake McDonald Lodge. From the lodge parking area, go about 6 miles on the Going to the Sun Road until reaching the Avalanche Lake TH. Once on the trail, go a little over 2 miles to reach the foot of the frozen lake.

- First few miles on the road can be busy and snow likely packed and icy unless a recent fresh snow.
- Boots with spikes and/or snow shoes are good if no fresh snow and it is packed and crunchy. Poles are helpful. Stay off cross country ski tracks as best you can unless you are skiing.
- Typically you will find some other tracks up to the lake to follow. The trail is fairly easy to navigate especially if you are familiar with it already.
- This trail can be very busy in the summer, but in the winter time you can enjoy the trail and lake all to yourself.
- Nice views of Upper McDonald Creek. You may see moose and deer along the road near the creek.

Approximate GPS data:
16.5 mile OB
950 ft ascend
6.5 hours

Getting to the TH: Park at Lake McDonald Lodge parking nearest Going to the Sun Road. Bathrooms are in this the parking area.

Fish Lake

Overview: 5.5 mile OB. Start up the Sperry Chalet trail and continue pass both left forks for Mt Brown and Snyder lake trails at 1.6 and 1.7 miles. At about 1.8 miles you cross the bridge at Snyder Creek and go right for Fish Lake.

- A shorter hike option from Lake McDonal Lodge.
- Plenty of trees and shade for this hike.
- Most of the hard climbing is in the first 1.5 miles.
- Expect bugs and mosquitoes at the lake. Nice winter hike option… and no mosquitoes. For winter, recommend shoe spikes and poles if packed and icy (or snow shoes if fresher snow).

Getting to the TH: Park at Lake McDonald Lodge parking nearest Going to the Sun Road. Sperry Chalet TH is just across the road and there are bathrooms in the parking area.

Approximate GPS data:
5.5 mile OB
1250 ft ascend
2.25 hours

Grinnell Glacier Overlook from The Loop

Overview: 11.25 mile OB starting at The Loop TH. At about 3.5 miles stay right heading to Granite Park Chalet where you eventually intersect with the Highline trail at about 4 miles. Take a right on the Highline trail for a short distance to a marked left fork that climbs steeply up to Grinnell Glacier Overlook.

- Nice views of Grinnell Glacier, Upper Grinnell Lake, The Salamander Glacier, and the smaller Gem Glacier.
- Most of the climbing is in first 4 miles to the Highline trail intersection. Steady grade but not killer steep. Climbing from the Highline Trail to the OL is quite steep and an effort.

- Can be windy and cool at the OL. Consider taking a warm hat, gloves, and hooded parka or wind breaker.
- Use trekking poles to help with the climbing and descending.
- Trails are in great shape.

Getting to the TH: Continue on Going to the Sun Road past Lake McDonald towards Logan Pass. Park at The Loop TH at 1st hairpin corner. Parking can go quick. TH has bathrooms.

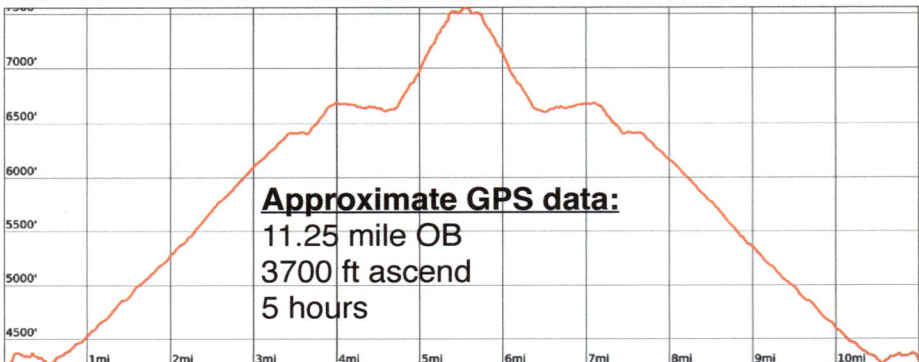

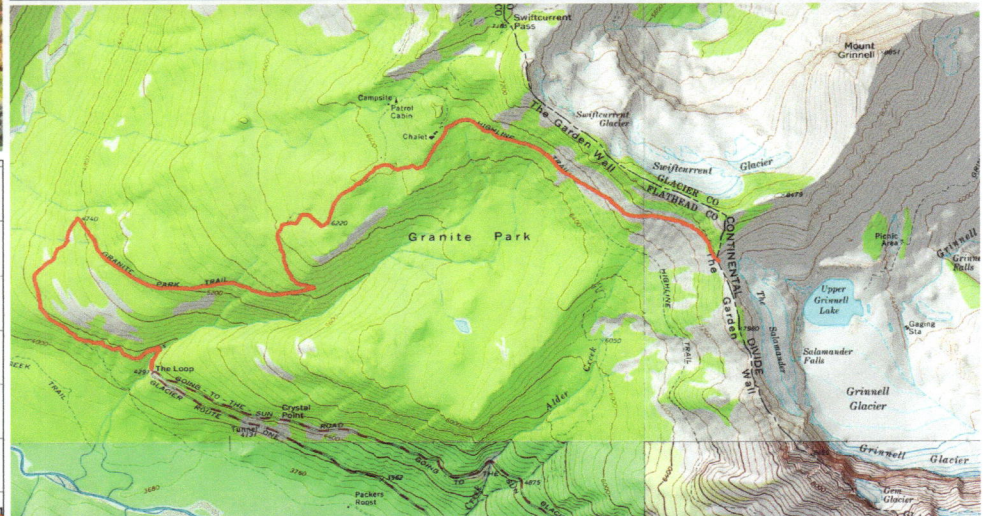

Approximate GPS data:
11.25 mile OB
3700 ft ascend
5 hours

Gunsight Lake and Pass

Overview: 18 mile OB from Gunsight Pass TH. 12 mile OB to Gunsight Lake is a shorter option.
* Recommend late summer or early fall as hazardous snow fields can persist on the east side of the pass.
* Views of Jackson Glacier and Blackfoot Glacier.
* Can be very buggy, especially around Gunsight Lake.
* Thick chest high brush in a number of areas.
* Can have a lot of sun exposure.
* Recommend early start.
* Bring plenty of nutrition and drinks.
* Use the shuttle or two cars to make a 20 mile PTP hike over to Sperry Chalet and down to Lake McDonald Lodge.

Getting to the TH: Gunsight Pass TH is marked and near Jackson Glacier Overlook on Going to the Sun Road past Logan Pass heading east before you reach St. Mary Lake.

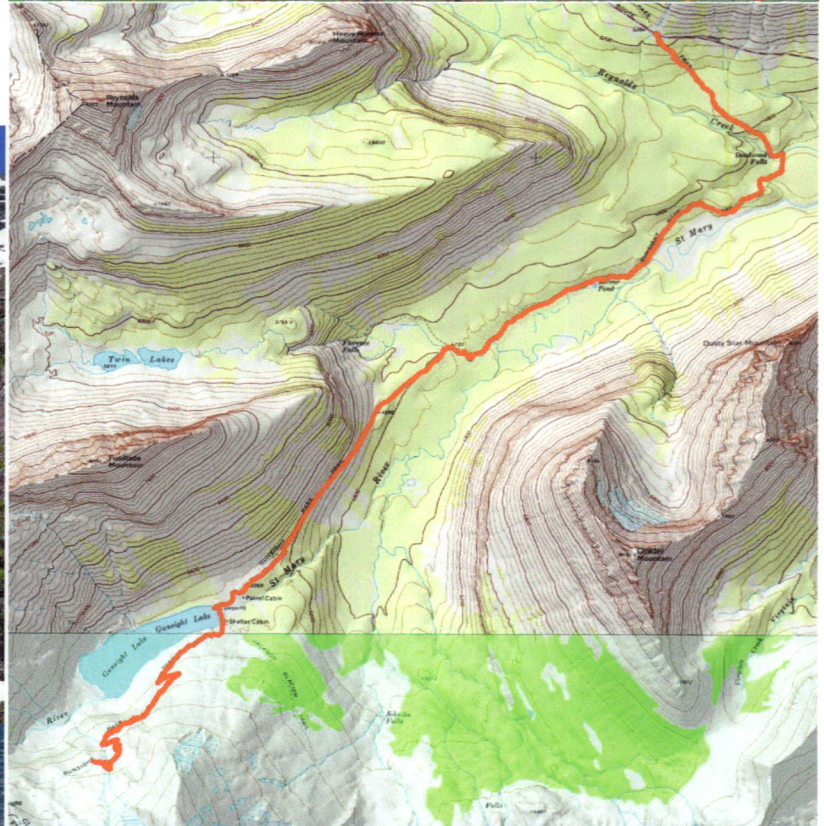

Approximate GPS data:
18 mile OB
3750 ft ascend
9 hours

Gunsight Pass from Lake McDonald

Overview: 22 mile OB. Hike about 6 miles to Sperry Chalet and continue past this for a short climb over Lincoln Pass. Proceed down and along Lake Ellen Wilson. At the end of the lake you have to cross Lincoln Creek. Trekking poles proved useful crossing this creek. Then you have a short climb to Gunsight Pass and awesome views both sides including Gunsight Lake on the far side of the Pass.

- The Lake McDonald approach melts sooner than coming from other side of Gunsight Pass. Recommend mid July and later but check trail conditions with park rangers. Snow hazards can persist into August on the other side of Gunsight Pass.
- Nice views from Sperry Chalet onward.
- Start early when cool for initial climb to Sperry Chalet.

- Hardest grades are really the first 1.5 miles or so.
- Very likely to see Mt Goats from Sperry Chalet onward.
- Pack plenty of nutrition and water.
- Shorter option is going to view points of Lake Ellen Wilson.
- If you make reservations at Sperry Chalet, make shorter day trips.
- Slightly shorter 20 mile PTP hike going from Gunsight Pass TH on other side of Logan Pass and down to Lake McDonald Lodge. Shuttle required or multiple cars. Check trail and snow conditions to determine if you can pass.

Getting to the TH: Park at Lake McDonald Lodge parking nearest Going to the Sun Road. Sperry Chalet TH is just across the road and there are bathrooms in the parking area.

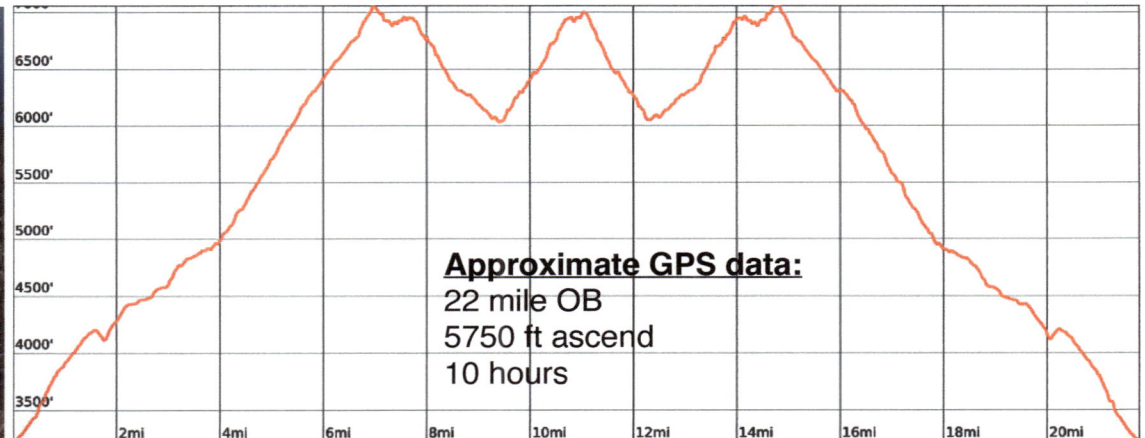

Approximate GPS data:
22 mile OB
5750 ft ascend
10 hours

Hidden Lake Overlook & Lake

Overview: 5.6 mile OB to the lake. Shorter option to overlook is 2.9 mile OB.
- Popular trail and heavy traffic typically to and from overlook.
- Scenic views and wildflowers.
- May see plenty of animals including: Mt Goats, Bighorn Sheep, Marmots and Grizzly Bears.

Getting to the TH: Take Going to the Sun Road to Logan Pass Visitor Center. Trail begins up the stairs next to the visitor center. Bathrooms are available below the visitor center.

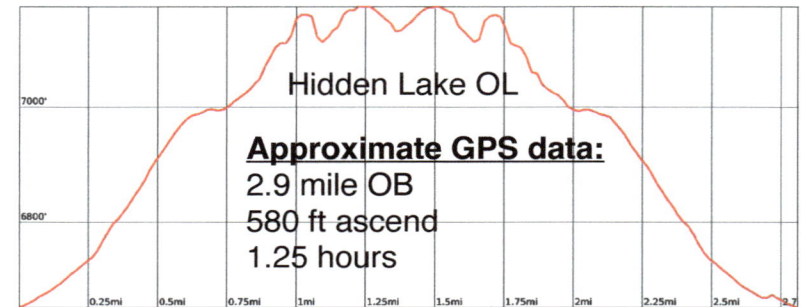

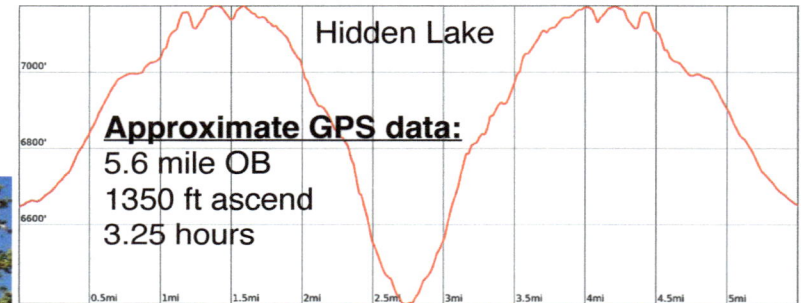

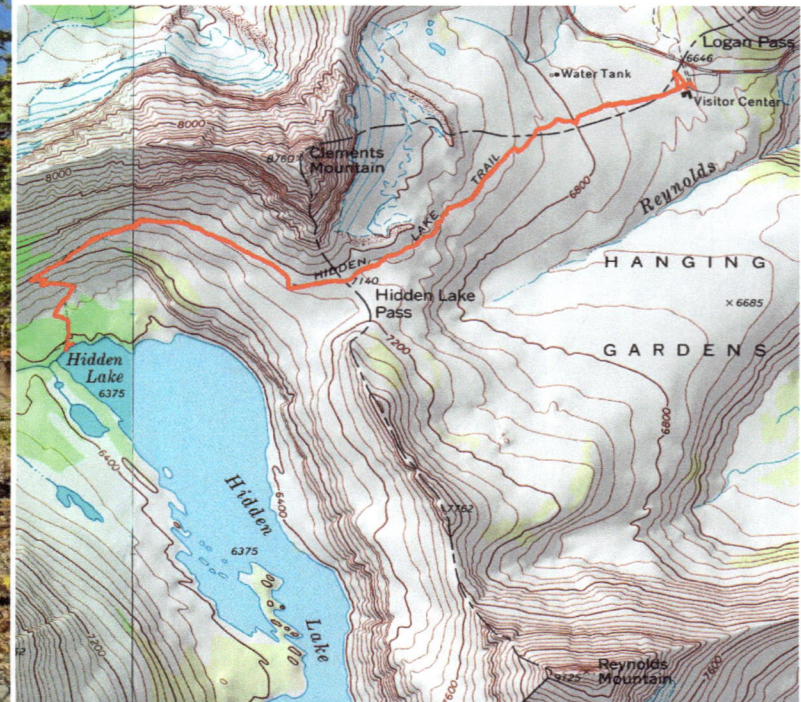

Hidden Lake OL

Approximate GPS data:
2.9 mile OB
580 ft ascend
1.25 hours

Hidden Lake

Approximate GPS data:
5.6 mile OB
1350 ft ascend
3.25 hours

Highline Trail & Grinnell Glacier Overlook

Overview: 15.5 mile OB to Grinnell Glacier OL. 1.5 mile RT extension to include Granite Park Chalet for a 17 mile OB total. At about mile 6.8 is the marked fork for the Grinnell Glacier OL trail and is about 0.85 miles uphill (this grade is quite steep and a very good work out, trekking poles highly recommended). Views are worth it.

• Views of Grinnell Glacier, Salamander Glacier, Gem Glacier, and Upper Grinnell Lake.
• Popular trail and can be busy.
• Recommend starting early for parking and to get a head of the crowds.
• Scenic views and wildflowers.
• Shorter PTP option if using a shuttle, is to proceed 4 miles downhill from Granite Park Chalet to The Loop TH. Overall PTP is about 13.5 miles (includes Grinnell Glacier OL).

Getting to the TH: Take Going to the Sun Road to Logan Pass Visitor Center. Take the sidewalk over to the crosswalk on Going to Sun Road. TH starts just across the road. Bathrooms are available below the visitor center.

Approximate GPS data:
15.5 mile OB to Grinnell Glacier OL
17.0 mile OB includes Granite Park Chalet
3000 ft ascend, 7.5 hours

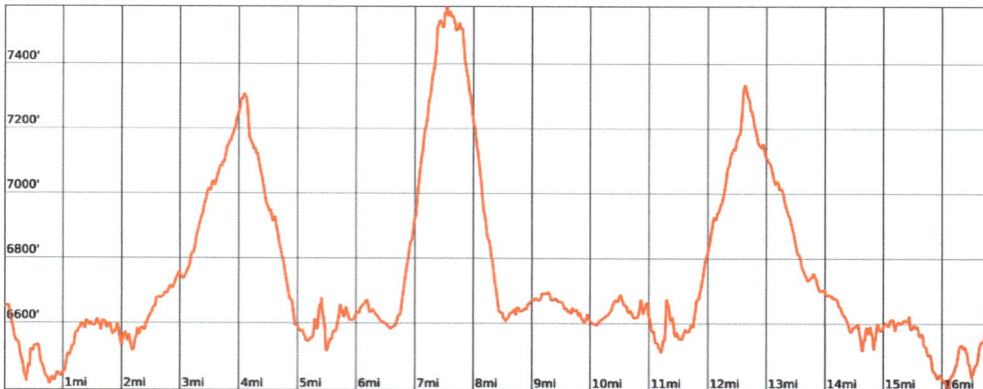

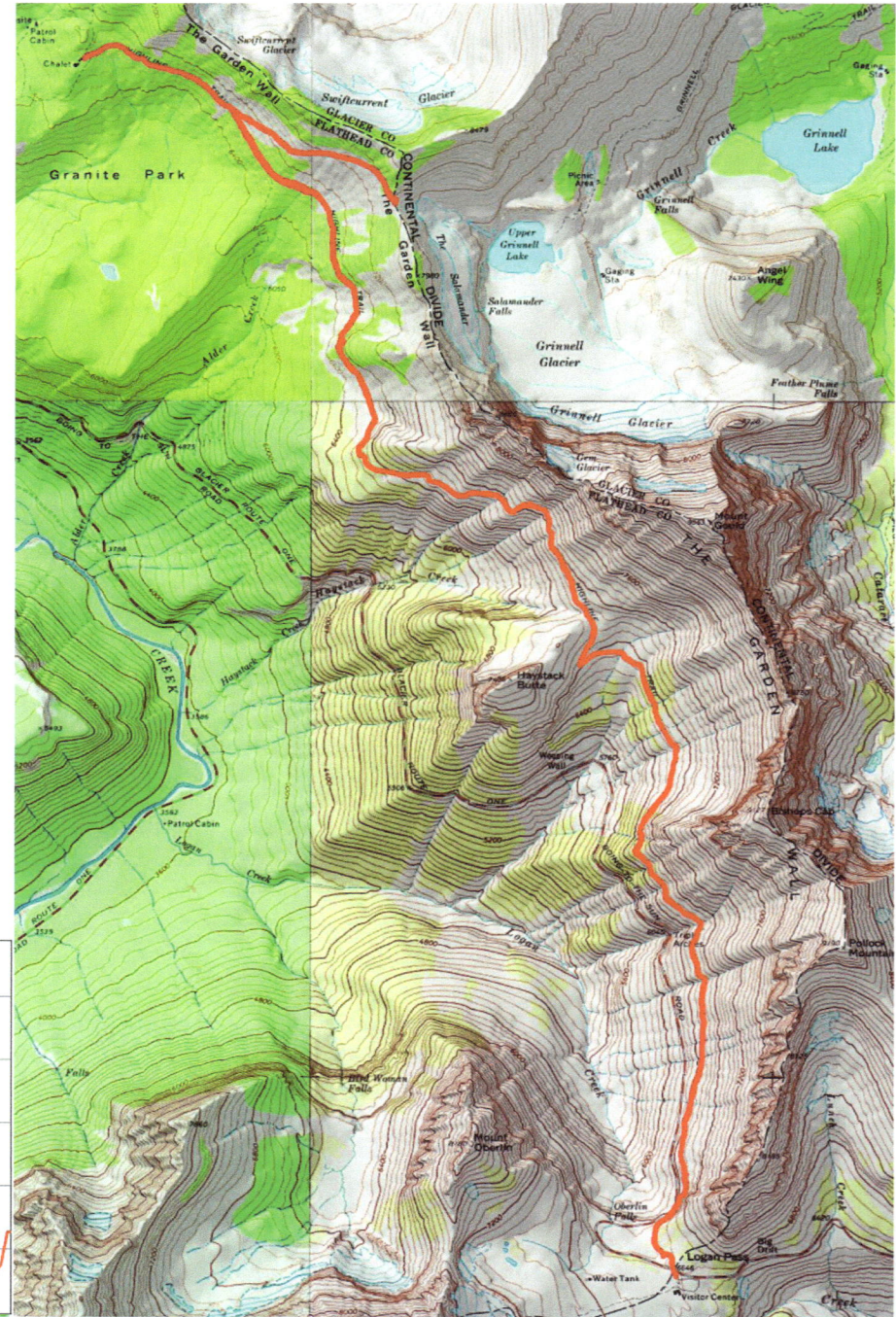

Howe Lake

Overview: 3.25 mile OB to the first lake.
- Trail is through an old burn area and has a lot of sun exposure.
- Mostly rolling terrain with slight grades.
- Not a lot of parking so trail isn't too busy.

Getting to the TH:
- Take a left on Camas Road shortly after West Entrance at the Apgar intersection.
- Then take right to Fish Creek Campground and proceed past day use and camp areas staying left until dirt road.
- Stay right on narrow dirt road past large dirt parking area for Rocky Point TH which is just past the Fish Creek Campground paved area.
- Continue about 5.5 miles on the rough narrow dirt road (Inside North Fork Road heading towards Polebridge) to marked TH. You will pass Howe Ridge TH sign.
- TH probably has room for approximately 5-6 cars.

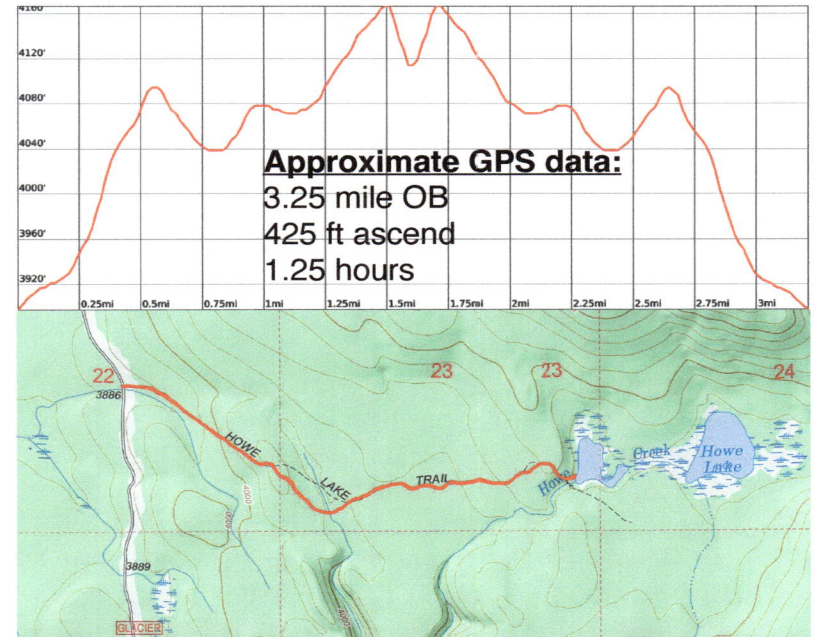

Approximate GPS data:
3.25 mile OB
425 ft ascend
1.25 hours

Huckleberry Lookout

Overview: 11.75 mile OB.
- Nice views up the North Folk and looking east across the valley towards Glacier Park Mountains.
- Trail is in great shape with fairly easy steady grade.
- A lot of shade down lower and more open near lookout with views.
- Buggy.
- You might see a bear.
- Nice wild flowers in June-July.
- Trail can get busy later in the day.

Getting to the TH: Take a left at the Apgar intersection on Camas Road heading towards Polebridge. Marked TH pullout is on left after 5-6 miles. Arrive early since only about 7 official parking spots. People do parallel park on Camas Road.

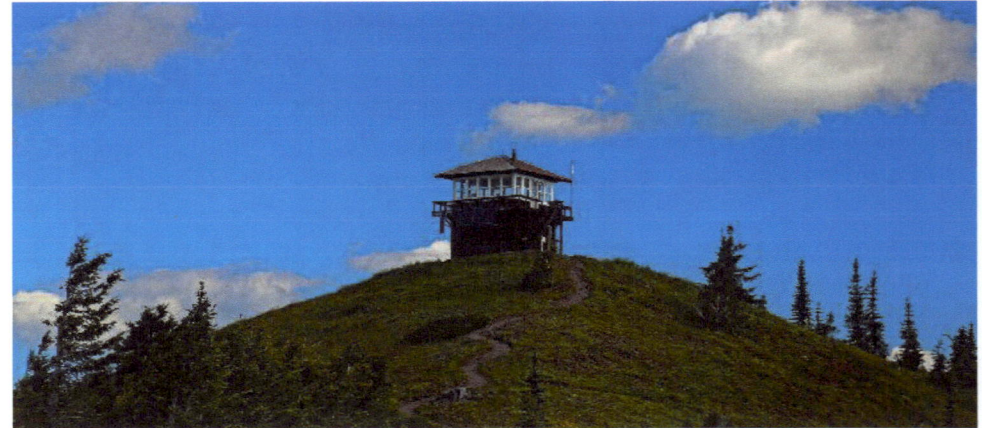

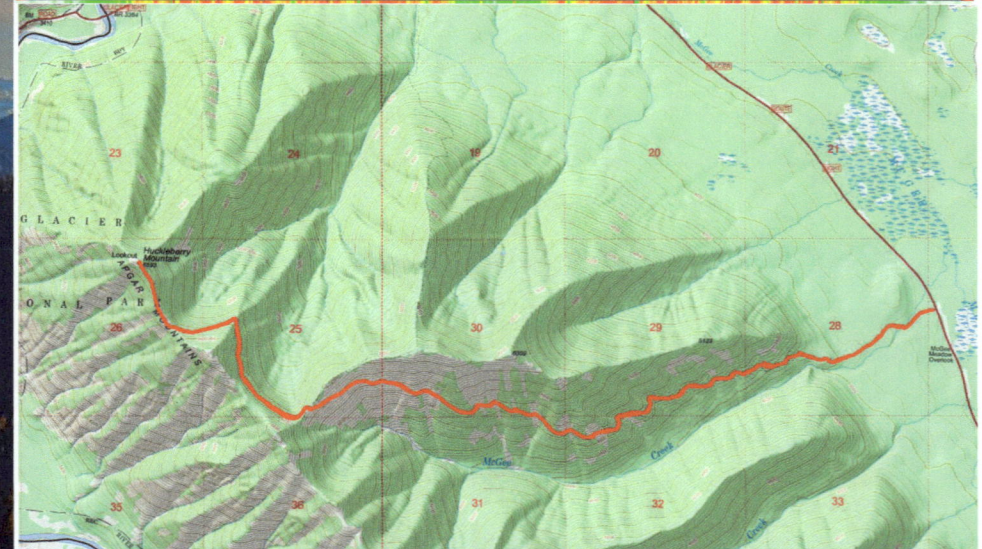

Approximate GPS data:
11.75 mile OB
2780 ft ascend
5.5 hours

Johns Lake Loop (Winter Edition)

Overview: 5.25 mile loop. In the winter the Going to the Sun Road is closed at Lake McDonald Lodge. From the lodge parking area, go about 1.4 miles on the Going to the Sun Road until reaching the marked TH sign for Johns Lake trail on the right. The trail goes by Johns Lake before exiting back out on to the Going to the Sun Road. Across the road is the footbridge over Upper McDonald Creek. Proceed along Upper McDonald Creek trail towards Lake McDonald until you reach the North Lake McDonald Road. Go left on the road a short distance until reaching the Going to the Sun Road again. Take a right to head back to the parking at the lodge.

- The Going to the Sun Road can be busy and snow likely packed and icy unless a recent fresh snow.
- Boots with spikes and/or snow shoes work well.
- Awesome views along Upper McDonald Creek.
- If doing the loop in the summer it is about 2.1 miles and you can park where the Going to the Sun Road intersects with North Lake McDonald Road.

Getting to the TH: Park at Lake McDonald Lodge parking nearest Going to the Sun Road. Bathrooms are nearby.

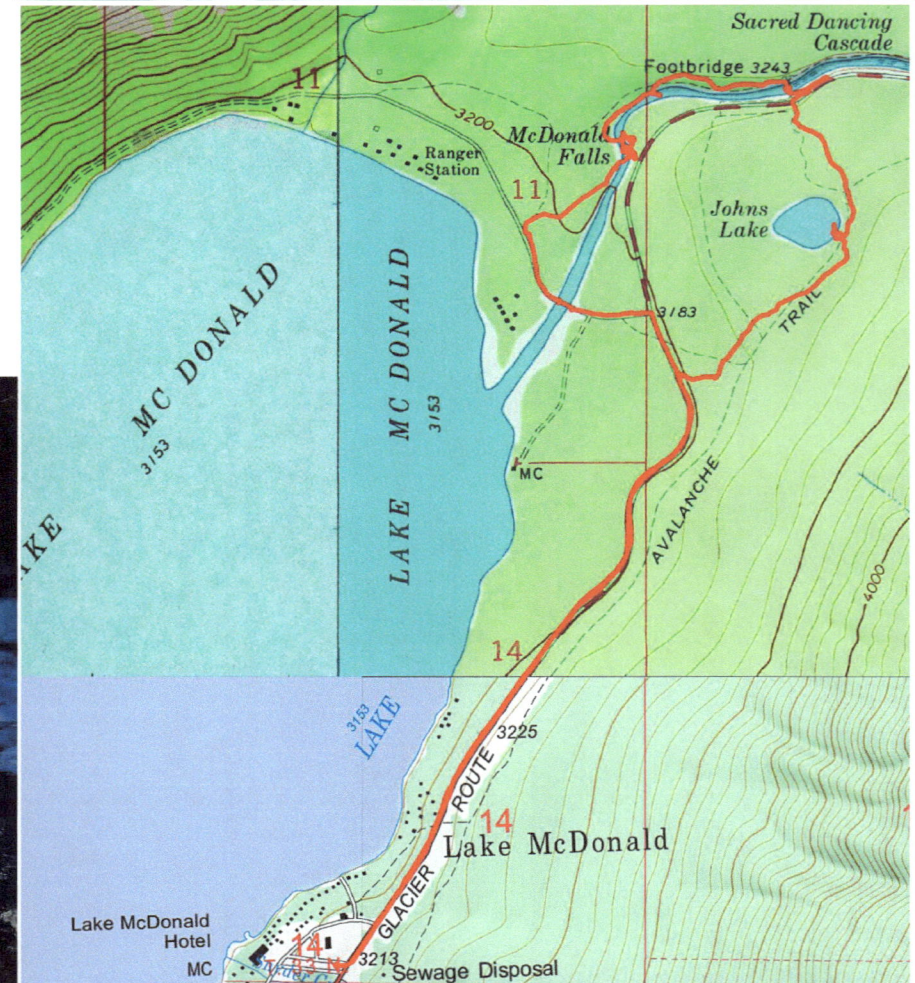

Approximate GPS data:
5.25 mile loop
280 ft ascend
2.5 hours

Mount Brown Lookout

Overview: 10.3 mile OB. Start on the Sperry Chalet TH, after about 1.6 miles is the marked left fork for the Mt Brown Lookout trail. Recommend some uphill fitness before attempting this hike.

- Awesome views!
- The first 1.6 miles from the TH are the warmup 😀.
- Once on the Mt Brown Lookout trail the grades are fairly steep and steady. A good workout but views are worth it.
- I counted 29 switchbacks once on the Mt. Brown LO trail.
- Recommend trekking poles to aid in both going up and down.
- Can be breezy and cool at top. Bring layers, hat and gloves.
- May see Mt Goats, and in the fall you might see migrating Golden Eagles soaring and heading south. Oct 6, 2020 I saw 10-20 Golden Eagles in about 30 minutes from a view point several switchbacks down from the LO (switchback #25).

Getting to the TH: Park at Lake McDonald Lodge parking nearest Going to the Sun Road. Sperry Chalet TH is just across the road and there are bathrooms in the parking area.

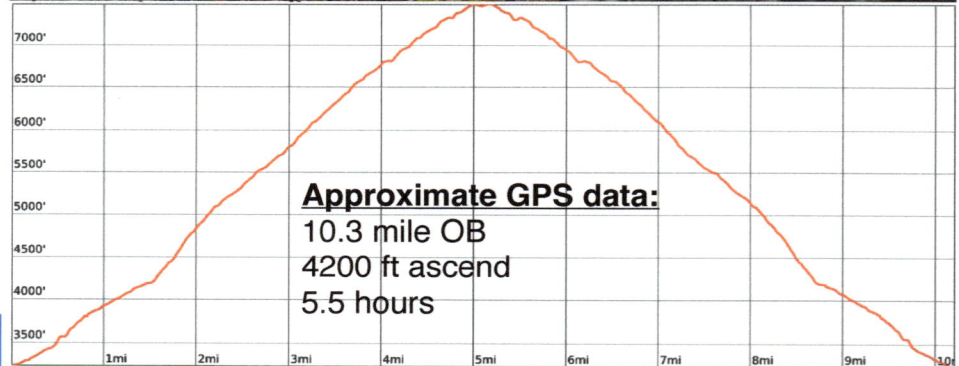

Approximate GPS data:
10.3 mile OB
4200 ft ascend
5.5 hours

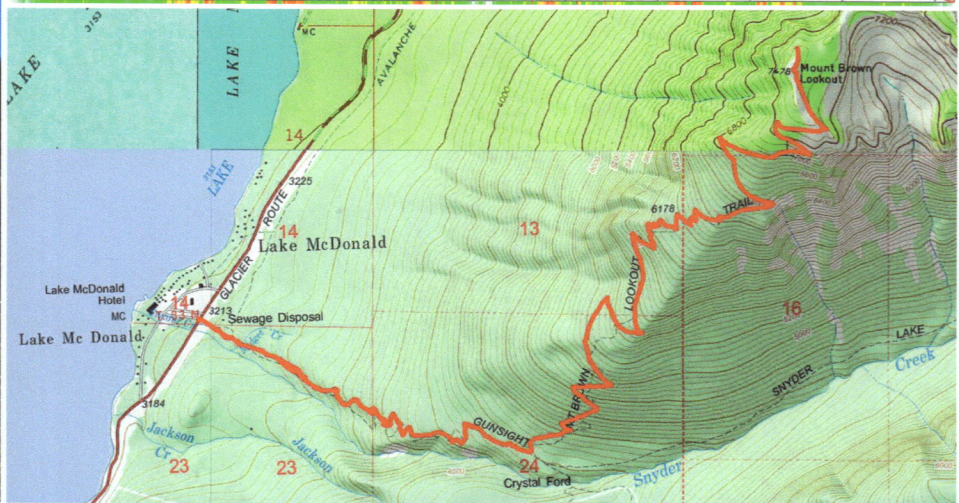

Mount Oberlin Summit

Overview: 3.5 mile OB. Once on the slopes of Mt Oberlin at a little over 1 mile the trail gets pretty steep and is a good workout. It is not a maintained trail and can be a little crude. At about 1.2 miles there is a fork at the base of an open slope with loose rock. Good views staying left, although I generally take the right fork and traverse back across the rocky slope. Then it proceeds fairly straight up to the top with steep zig zags and loose rocks.

- Good work out but the 360° views at the top are worth it.
- Plenty of wild flowers down low, a waterfall and you may see Mt Goats and Bighorn Sheep.
- Highly recommend trekking poles to aid in going up and down and help to prevent slipping on loose rocks and gravel.
- Recommend good traction shoes.
- I'm not a technical climber and do not consider this a requirement for this hike. Although I do recommend some level of fitness for this hike.
- Can be windy and cool on the top.
- Since you already have the parking spot, do this hike early when it is cool and then proceed to Hidden Lake or the Overlook after a lunch break.

Getting to the TH: Take Going to the Sun Road to Logan Pass Visitor Center. Take the sloped winding sidewalk to the right of the visitor center and the stairs. The trail starts on the right from this sidewalk heading through a meadow. If you reach the visitor center you went too far and need to back track down the sloped sidewalk a few yards. Bathrooms are available below the visitor center.

The trail may have a sign in front of it and be roped off (see photo), but you can hike it just stay on the trail. If you have questions just ask a ranger at the visitor center...I did and have hiked this several times.

Approximate GPS data:
3.5 mile OB
1550 ft ascend
2.5 hours

Piegan Pass from Siyeh Bend

Overview: 10.0 mile OB. Siyeh Bend provides access to both Piegan and Siyeh Passes. Trails are well marked.
- Trails in great shape and steady with gradual grades.
- Plenty of wild flowers.
- Views of Piegan Glacier, and in the distance on the left you can see Jackson Glacier and Blackfoot Glacier.
- Continue over the pass a little ways for better views looking north towards Many Glacier.
- Make a reservation at Many Glacier Hotel and continue over the pass and return the next day or organize a shuttle.

Getting to the TH: Take Going to the Sun road over Logan Pass for a little over 2 miles before reaching marked TH at Siyeh Bend. Multiple pullouts on both sides of road. Trail begins on right side of the Siyeh Creek Bridge.

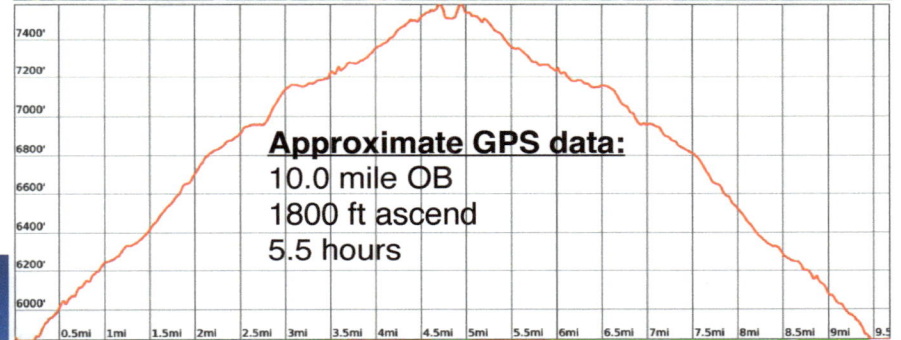

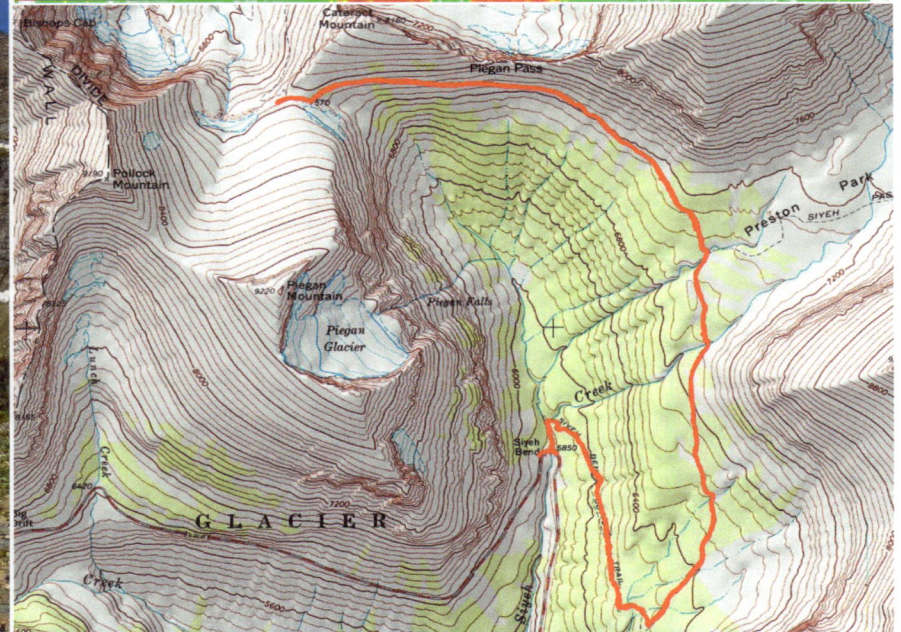

Approximate GPS data:
10.0 mile OB
1800 ft ascend
5.5 hours

Rocky Point (winter hike option)

Overview: 5.9 mile OB to Rocky Point, shorter 3.6 mile OB to Fish Creek Campground. Start at the gate on Grist road which eventually turns into the Fish Creek bike path. The path intersects with the Fish Creek CG road which you continue on to the picnic area for lake views. Continue to end of picnic area along Fish Creek and cross foot bridge on the right. Proceed past Amphitheater towards the lake shore through camp site loop D where the trail to Rocky Point starts just up from the shoreline. Continue around the bay past the boat house to Rocky Point for more views.

- In the winter Camas and Grist roads gated and closed.
- Popular and can be snow packed. Use boots and possibly traction devices if icy. If fresh snow, snowshoes or skis are a good option.
- Mostly flat and rolling gradual climbs.
- Nice views of Lake McDonald looking towards Mt. Brown.

Getting to the TH: Turn left on Camas road at the Apgar intersection and head towards Fish Creek CG. Just after crossing McDonald Creek bridge and before winter gate on Camas road, take right to a small winter parking area where Grist Road is gated and closed.

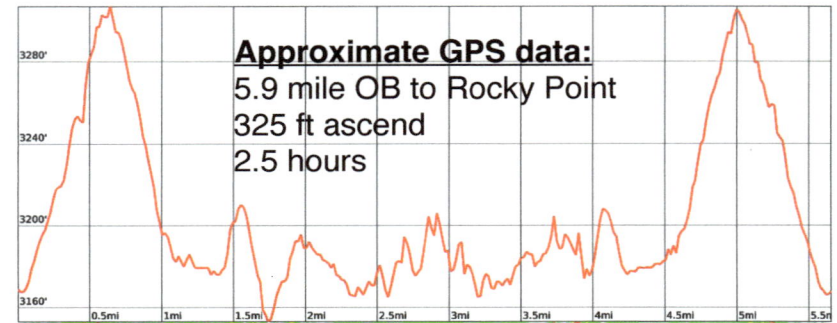

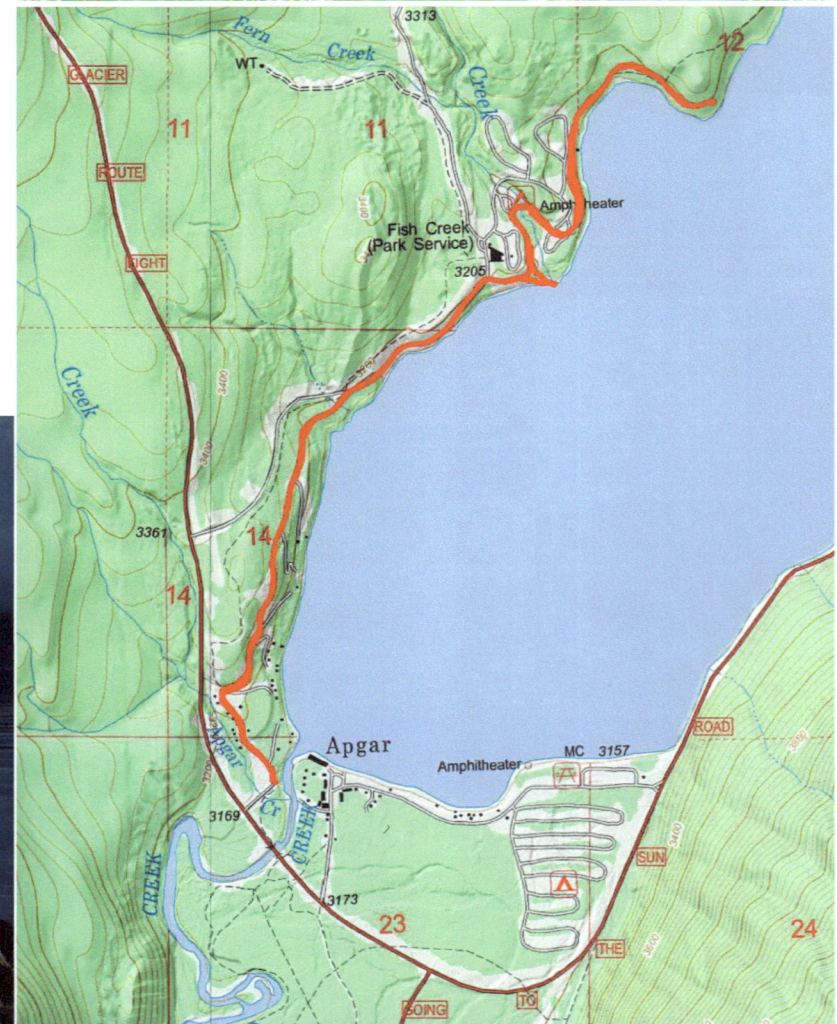

Approximate GPS data:
5.9 mile OB to Rocky Point
325 ft ascend
2.5 hours

Siyeh Pass from Siyeh Bend

Overview: 10.1 mile OB. Siyeh Bend provides access to both Piegan and Siyeh Passes. Trails are well marked.

- Trails in great shape and steady with gradual grades for the first 3.6 miles and then gets a bit steeper on the switchbacks until you reach the pass.
- Plenty of wild flowers.
- Views of Piegan Glacier. Sexton Glacier can be seen from the other side of the pass.
- There is one crossing of Siyeh Creek that requires rock hopping if the water is running high earlier in the season. Trekking poles help.
- Can be windy and cooler on the pass.
- Option to make a 10.9 mile PTP by continuing down the other side of the pass to the TH at Sunrift Gorge. Shuttle required.

Getting to the TH: Take Going to the Sun road over Logan Pass for a little over 2 miles before reaching marked TH at Siyeh Bend. Multiple pullouts on both sides of road. Trail begins on right side of the Siyeh Creek Bridge.

Approximate GPS data:
10.1 mile OB
2250 ft ascend
4.75 hours

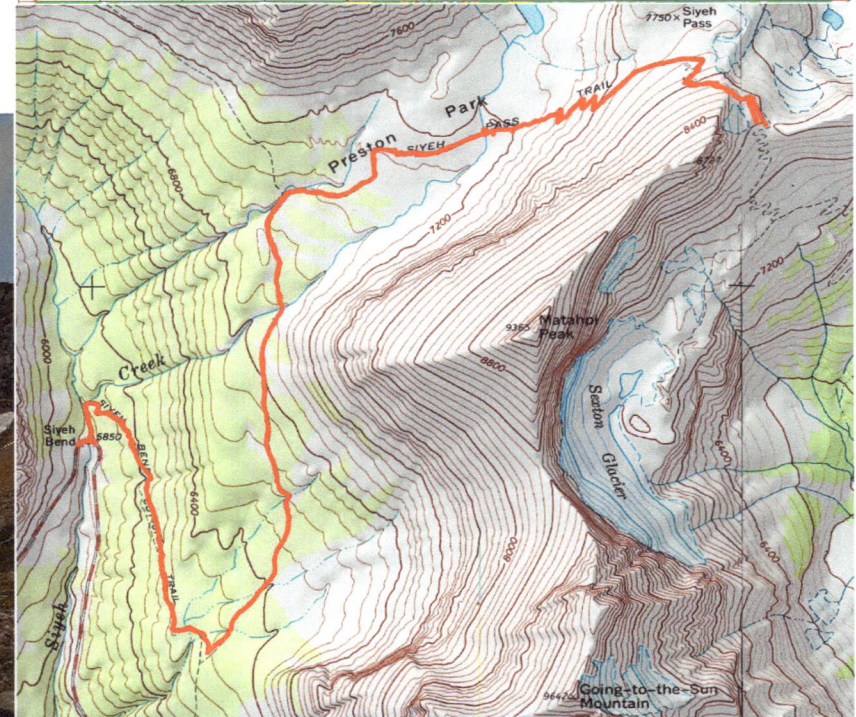

Siyeh Pass from Sunrift Gorge

Overview: 11.7 mile OB. TH at Sunrift Gorge near Saint Mary Lake.
- Trail in great shape and grades not too bad. As you approach the pass the switchbacks are a bit steeper.
- A lot of sun exposure since area had past fires making interesting landscapes.
- Views of Sexton Glacier and waterfalls.
- Can be windy and cooler at the pass.
- Option to make a 10.9 mile PTP by continuing over the pass to the TH at Siyeh Bend. Shuttle required.

Getting to the TH: Take Going to the Sun road over Logan Pass and proceed down towards Saint Mary Lake. There is a pullout at Sunrift Gorge on the right that is marked. It isn't a big pullout so get there early. The stairs going up the hill across the road is the TH.

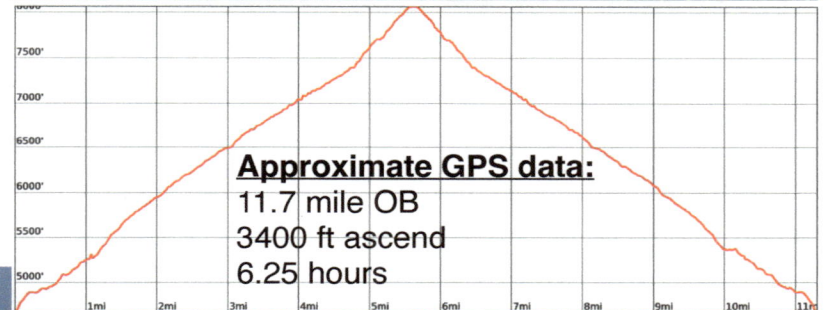

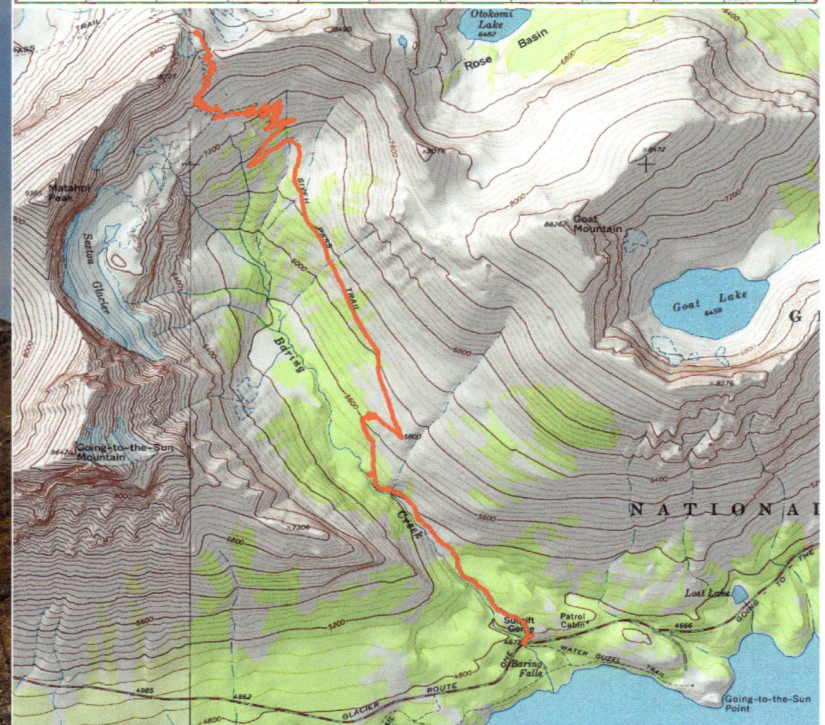

Approximate GPS data:
11.7 mile OB
3400 ft ascend
6.25 hours

Snyder Lake

Overview: 9 mile OB. Hike about 1.7 miles from TH to the marked left fork for Snyder Lake. The first 1.5 miles are the steepest, then grades fairly steady and easier.
- View of Little Matterhorn.
- Trail to Snyder Lake can be a little overgrown, wet and muddy in spots early in the season. I'd recommend fall or winter which is very scenic and fewer bugs.
- Can be buggy especially at the lake if no wind.

Getting to the TH: Park at Lake McDonald Lodge parking nearest Going to the Sun Road. Sperry Chalet TH is just across the road and there are bathrooms in the parking area.

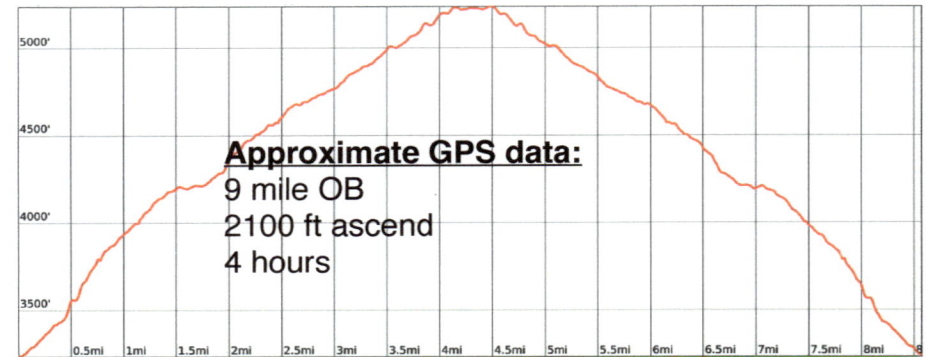

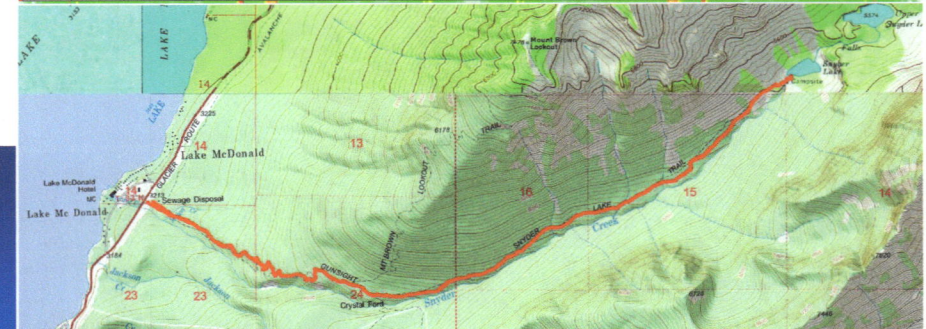

Approximate GPS data:
9 mile OB
2100 ft ascend
4 hours

Sperry Chalet & Lincoln Pass

Overview: 14.5 mile OB to Lincoln Pass. Shorter option is a little over 12 mile OB to Sperry Chalet. Begin on Sperry Chalet trail. At a little over 6 miles you arrive at Sperry Chalet and if you continue on for about 1 mile you climb up to Lincoln Pass.

- Views of Lake McDonald.
- Look for Mt Goats around Sperry Chalet and beyond.
- Make shorter day trips if you make reservations and stay at Sperry Chalet.
- First 1.5 miles has steeper grades, but then not bad.

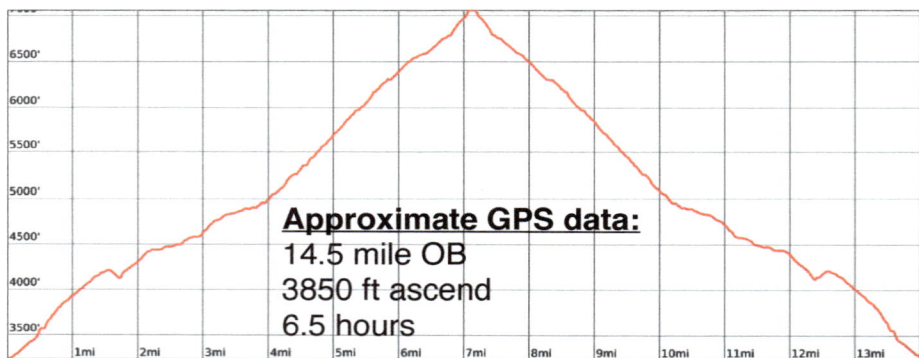

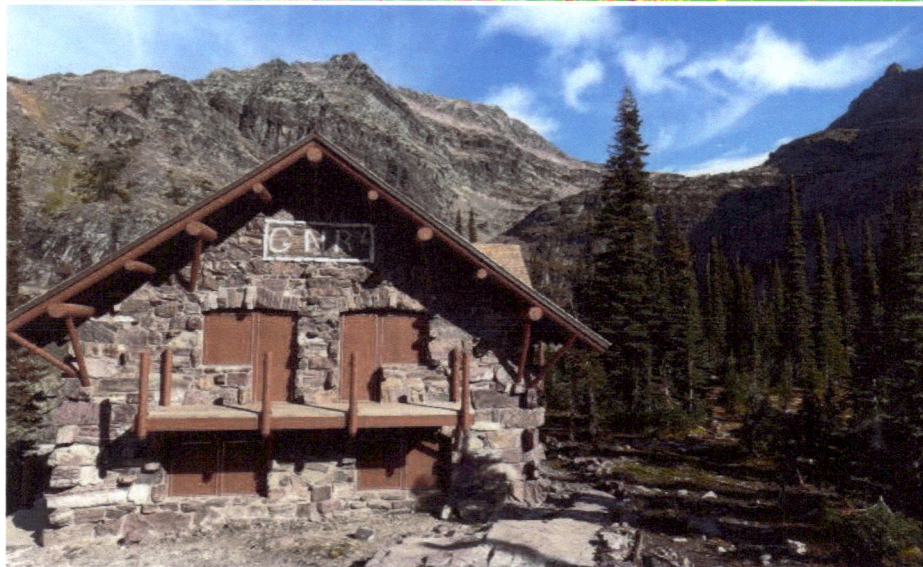

Getting to the TH: Park at Lake McDonald Lodge parking nearest Going to the Sun Road. Sperry Chalet TH is just across the road and there are bathrooms in the parking area.

Approximate GPS data:
14.5 mile OB
3850 ft ascend
6.5 hours

Sperry Glacier & Comeau Pass

Overview: 19.5 mile OB. Begin on Sperry Chalet trail. Soon after 6 miles (just below the Chalet) is a marked left fork for the Sperry Glacier trail. Once on the Sperry Glacier trail, 3 miles to Comeau Pass and 0.6 miles more to the glacier.

- Climb the stairs cut in the cliff to reach the pass.
- Look for Mt Goats around Sperry Chalet and beyond.
- Make shorter day trips if you make reservations and stay at Sperry Chalet.
- First 1.6 miles has steeper grades, but then not bad.
- Recommend starting early and complete first 6 miles (not too scenic) to the Chalet before too much sun or heat. Very scenic all the way on the Sperry Glacier trail!
- Make sure to pack enough food and drinks.
- Sperry Glacier trail can have snow hazards until later July or August, check with park rangers on conditions.

Getting to the TH: Park at Lake McDonald Lodge parking nearest Going to the Sun Road. Sperry Chalet TH is just across the road and there are bathrooms in the parking area.

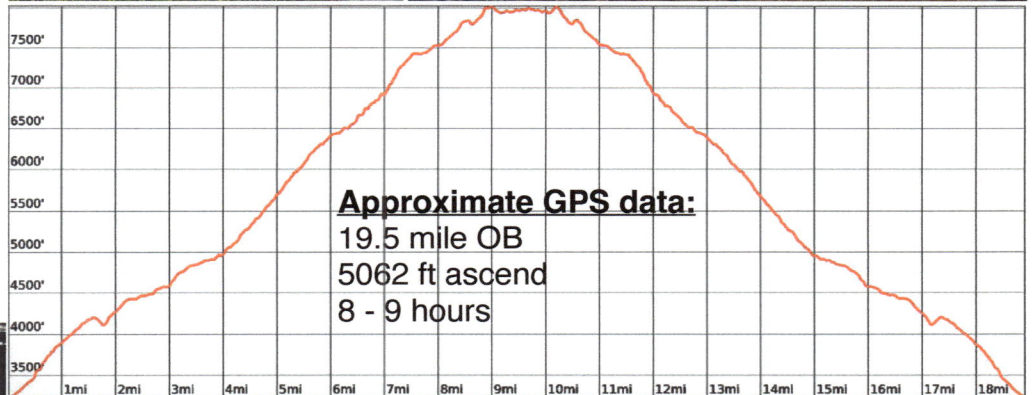

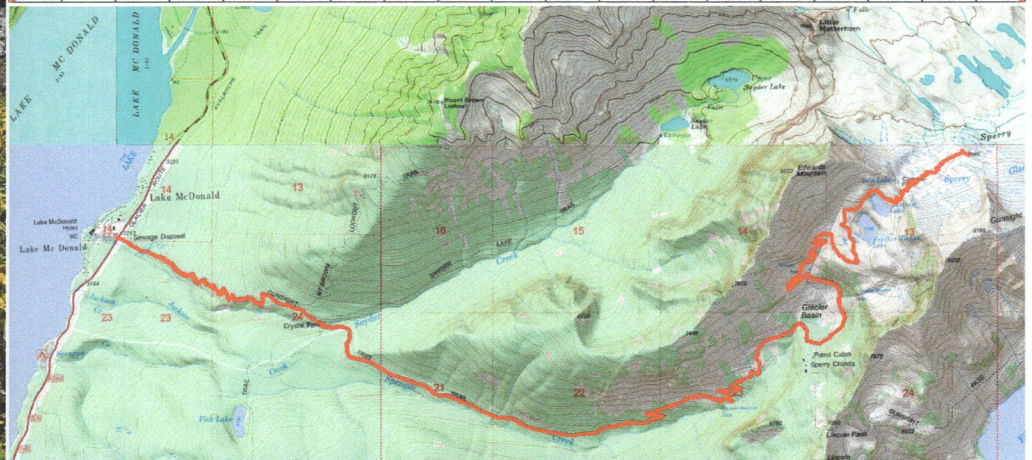

Approximate GPS data:
19.5 mile OB
5062 ft ascend
8 - 9 hours

Swiftcurrent Lookout from The Loop

Overview: 12.5 mile OB from The Loop TH. Start at The Loop TH and hike about 4 miles to Granite Park Chalet and Highline trail intersection. Go left on Highline trail heading north until right hand intersection for Swiftcurrent LO and Pass trail. Just before reaching the pass is the left fork to the LO.

- Incredible views from the lookout including Swiftcurrent Glacier. North Swiftcurrent Glacier can be seen from the LO.
- Start early for parking and to avoid the sun and heat during initial climb to chalet.
- Trails in great shape. Grades are steady and a workout, but not extreme. Not bad if cool.
- Bring plenty of liquids and nutrition.
- It can be cool and windy on top.

Getting to the TH: Continue on Going to the Sun Road past Lake McDonald towards Logan Pass. Park at The Loop TH at 1st hairpin corner. TH has bathrooms.

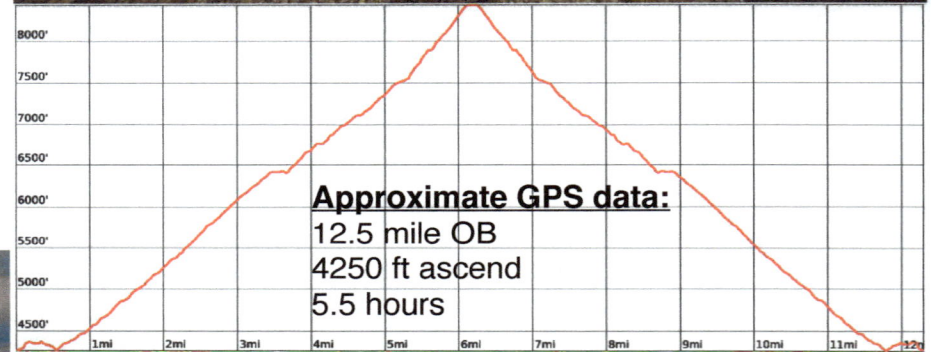

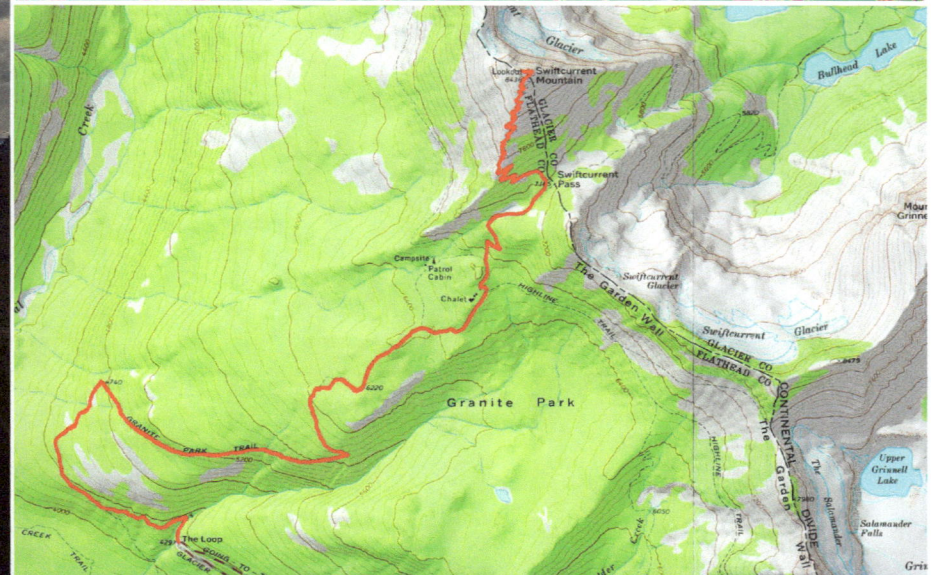

Approximate GPS data:
12.5 mile OB
4250 ft ascend
5.5 hours

Swiftcurrent Pass from The Loop

Overview: 10.5 mile OB from The Loop TH. Start at The Loop TH and hike about 4 miles to Granite Park Chalet and Highline trail intersection. Go left on Highline trail heading north until right hand intersection for Swiftcurrent LO and Pass trail. Continue straight past the left fork to Swiftcurrent LO. If you continue over the pass and down a short distance there is a crude right fork where you get views of Swiftcurrent Glacier on the right and views looking east towards Many Glacier. A good spot for a snack.

- Views of Swiftcurrent Glacier if you continue a short distance down from the pass towards Many Glacier.
- Start early for parking and to avoid the sun and heat during initial climb to chalet.
- Trails in great shape. Grades are steady and a workout, but not extreme. Not bad if cool.

Getting to the TH: Continue on Going to the Sun Road past Lake McDonald towards Logan Pass. Park at The Loop TH at 1st hairpin corner. TH has bathrooms.

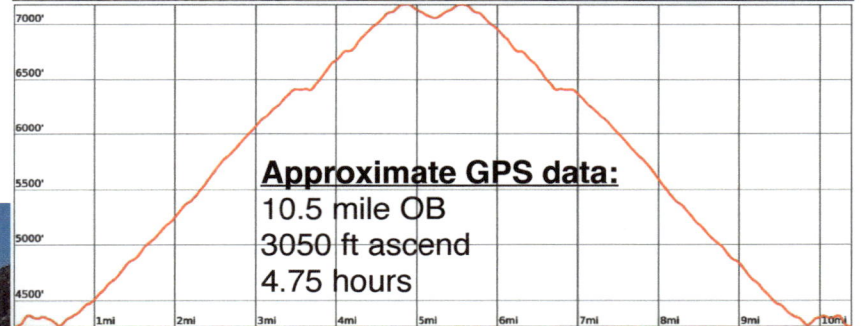

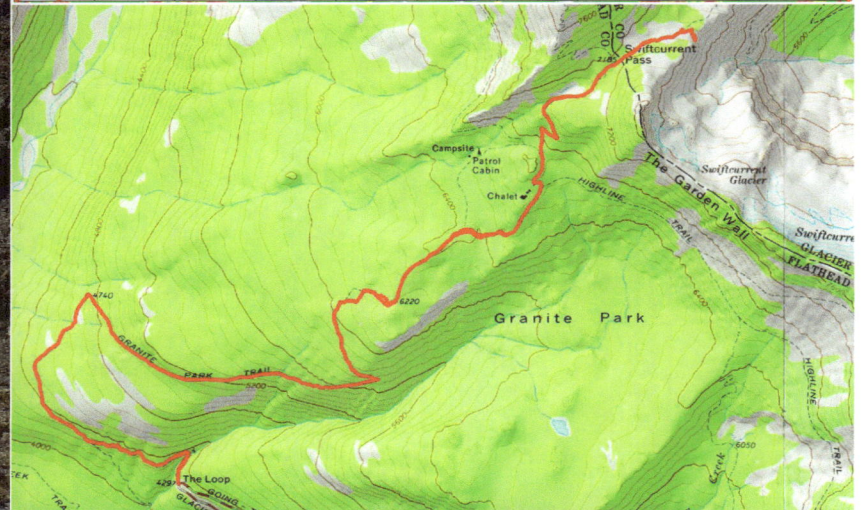

Approximate GPS data:
10.5 mile OB
3050 ft ascend
4.75 hours

Three Falls Trail from Sun Point: Baring Falls, St. Mary Falls, Virginia Falls

Overview: 6.7 mile OB from Sun Point. Trail is well marked and starts along St. Mary Lake. First you come to Baring Falls, followed by St. Mary Falls, and finally you climb some to get to Virginia Falls.
- Nice views of all three falls, and St. Mary Lake with surrounding Mountains.
- Trails in great shape and can be busy. Mostly flat and rolling grades. Some climbing towards Virginia Falls, but not much.
- I like this hike in the fall with the fall colors.

- Good hike and parking option since smaller parking areas along the Going to the Sun Road are busier and fill out quick.

Getting to the TH: Continue on Going to the Sun Road past Lake McDonald, over Logan Pass, and down towards St. Mary Lake. Take marked right hand turn to Sun Point which has picnic area and parking. The Three Falls TH is marked with a sign and located in a smaller parking area on the right as you enter. There are bathrooms on the edge of the larger parking area.

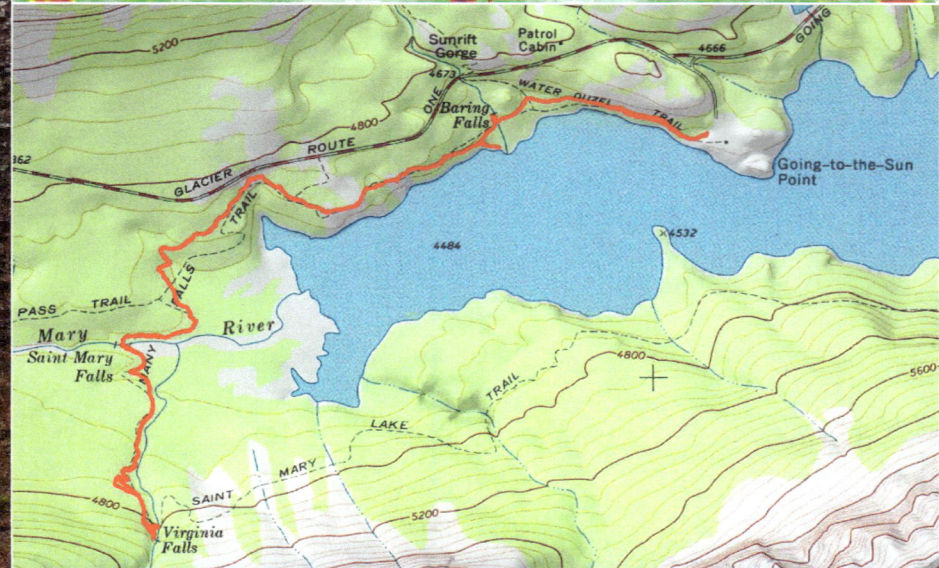

Approximate GPS data:
6.7 mile OB
850 ft ascend
2.5 hours

Upper McDonald Creek

Overview: 6.0 mile OB. Mostly flat with easy grades. Plenty of shade on this trail. Nice views of McDonald Creek.

Getting to the TH: Take a left at the end of Lake McDonald on North Lake McDonald Road and cross the bridge over McDonald Creek. The marked TH is on the right a short distance from the bridge.

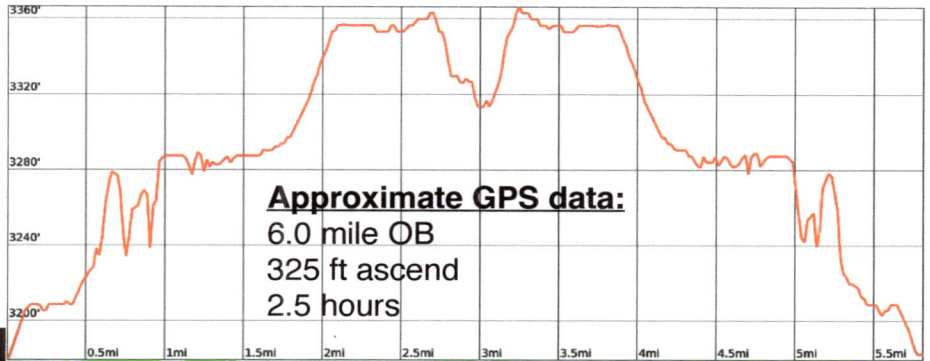

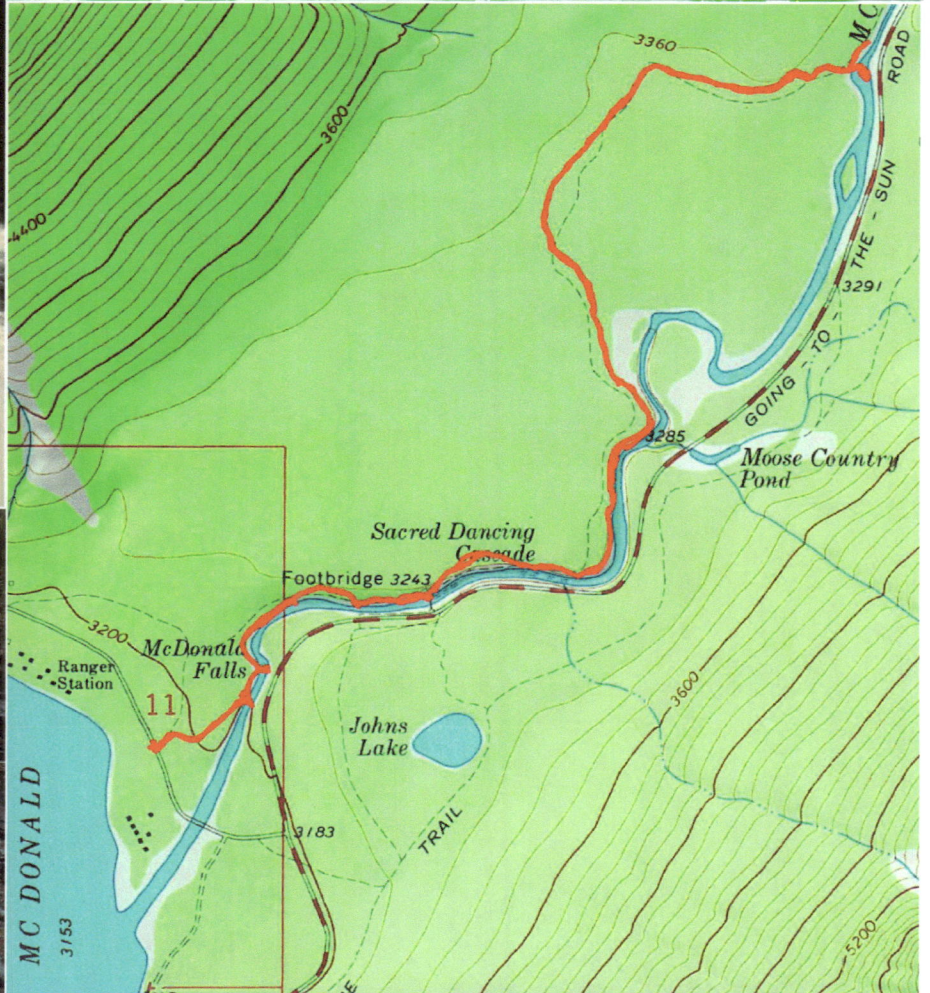

Approximate GPS data:
6.0 mile OB
325 ft ascend
2.5 hours

Glacier National Park - Two Medicine

Cobalt Lake

Overview: 12 mile OB. Start on the South Shore Trail near the Two Medicine Lake boat ramp area. This trail continues to Cobalt Lake and Two Medicine Pass. Rockwell falls view point is right off this trail. Trails and TH are well marked.

- Scenic trail with views along the way.
- Cobalt Lake and Rockwell Falls are very scenic.
- Look for wildlife. I've had numerous moose and bear sightings in the first few miles.
- Trail in excellent shape. Easy going first few miles, and a little steeper last couple of miles to the lake.
- Trail is busier around Two Medicine Lake, but as you get further along towards Cobalt Lake you may only see a few people.

Getting to the TH: Take Hwy 2 heading to East Glacier. Then take left heading north on MT-49. After about 4 miles, take a marked left on Two Medicine road heading to the park entrance and Two Medicine Lake. Stay left as you approach Two Medicine Lake and park near the boat ramp and dock. The marked South Shore TH starts on the left side of the dock near the shoreline. Bathrooms are near by.

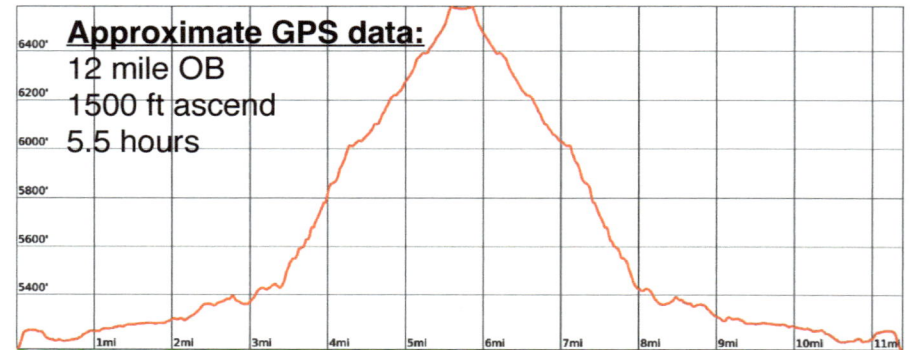

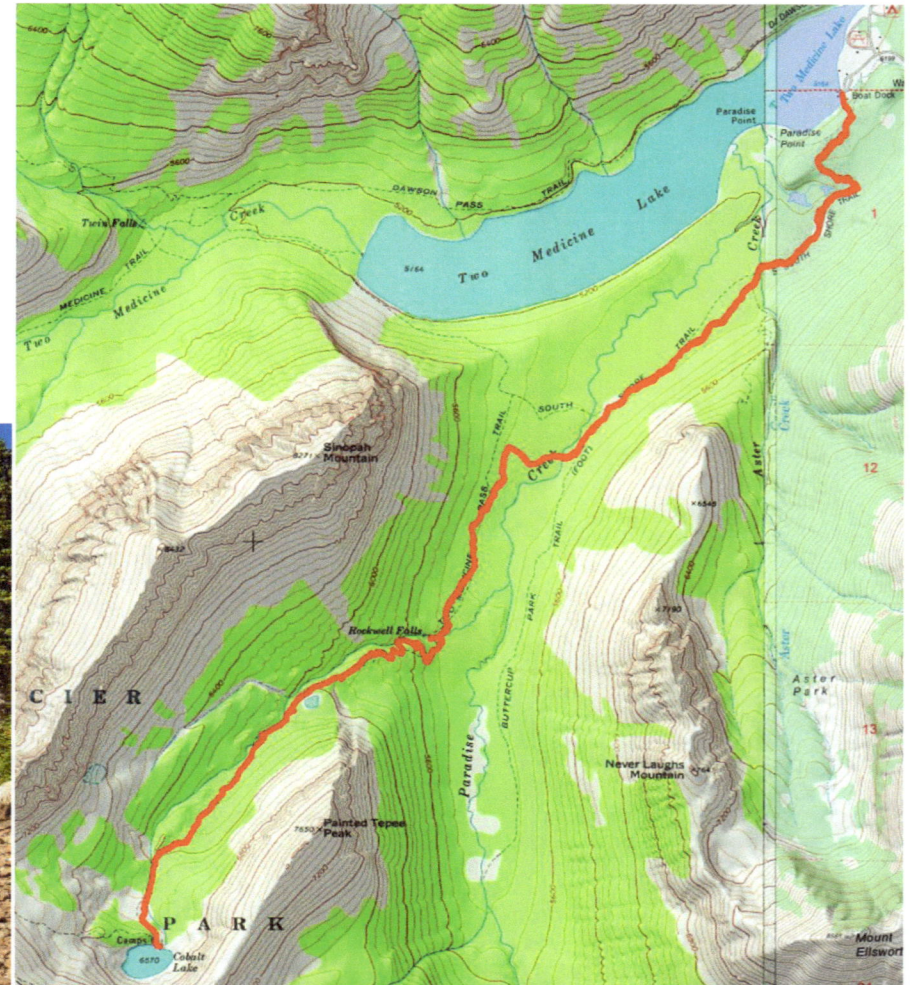

Approximate GPS data:
12 mile OB
1500 ft ascend
5.5 hours

Dawson Pass & No Name Lake

Overview: 14.3 mile OB. Trails and TH are well marked. Head north along the short path that follows the shore of Pray Lake, cross the foot bridge and in a short distance you come to a marked trail intersection. Go left to go to Dawson Pass. Hike about 3 miles along Two Medicine Lake which are mostly flat and easy. Stay right at marked intersection to go to No Name Lake and Dawson Pass. After over a mile of climbing there is a short left branch if you want to go to the shore of No Name Lake. Back track from No Name Lake and continue on to Dawson Pass.

- Nice views from the pass and along the trail including Two Medicine Lake, No Name Lake, and Pumpelly Pillar.
- Keep an eye out for moose and bears. I frequently see these on this trail.
- Trail in excellent shape. Easy going first few miles and mostly flat and rolling along Two Medicine Lake. Steeper grades and more of a workout as you head up to No Man Lake and then to Dawson Pass.
- Two Medicine area is frequently windy. It can be cool and breezy on the pass. Consider hooded jacket, warm hat and gloves.

- Great for fall colors, and plenty of flowers June-July.
- Take the Two Medicine Lake shuttle boat both ways to shorten hike by about 4 miles. Check for scheduling and tickets: glacierparkboats.com

Getting to the TH: Take Hwy 2 heading to East Glacier. Then take left heading north on MT-49. After about 4 miles, take a marked left on Two Medicine road heading to the park entrance and Two Medicine Lake. As you approach the Lake, take the first paved right at corner with Ranger Station towards day use and campsites. Continue through campsites until reaching day use parking slots on the Northeast side of Pray Lake for the North Shore TH. Bathrooms are near by.

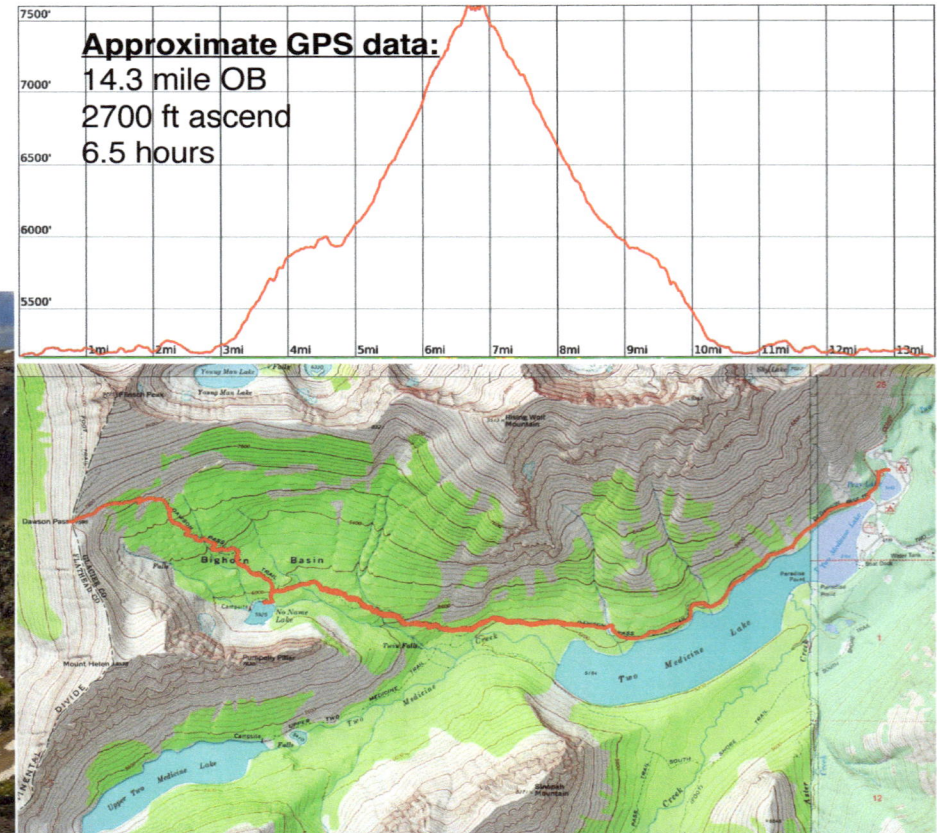

Approximate GPS data:
14.3 mile OB
2700 ft ascend
6.5 hours

Paradise Point & Aster Park Overlook

Overview: 4.6 mile OB. Start on the South Shore Trail near the Two Medicine Lake boat ramp area. After a short distance is a right fork to Paradise Point. Back track and then continue to left fork which climbs to Aster Park OL. The switchbacks on this climb are steeper but it isn't a long climb.

- Scenic views of Two Medicine.
- Look for wildlife. I've had numerous moose and bear sightings on this trail and not far from TH.
- Trail can be busy.
- Trails in excellent shape and well marked.

Getting to the TH: Take Hwy 2 heading to East Glacier. Then take left heading north on MT-49. After about 4 miles, take a marked left on Two Medicine road heading to the park entrance and Two Medicine Lake. Stay left as you approach Two Medicine Lake and park near the boat ramp and dock. The marked South Shore TH starts on the left side of the dock near the shoreline. Bathrooms are near by.

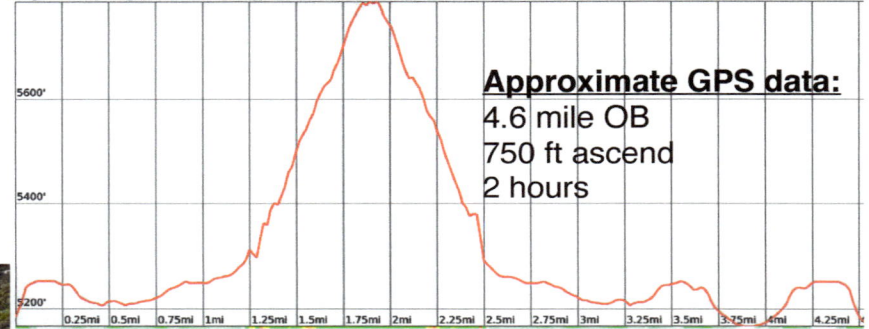

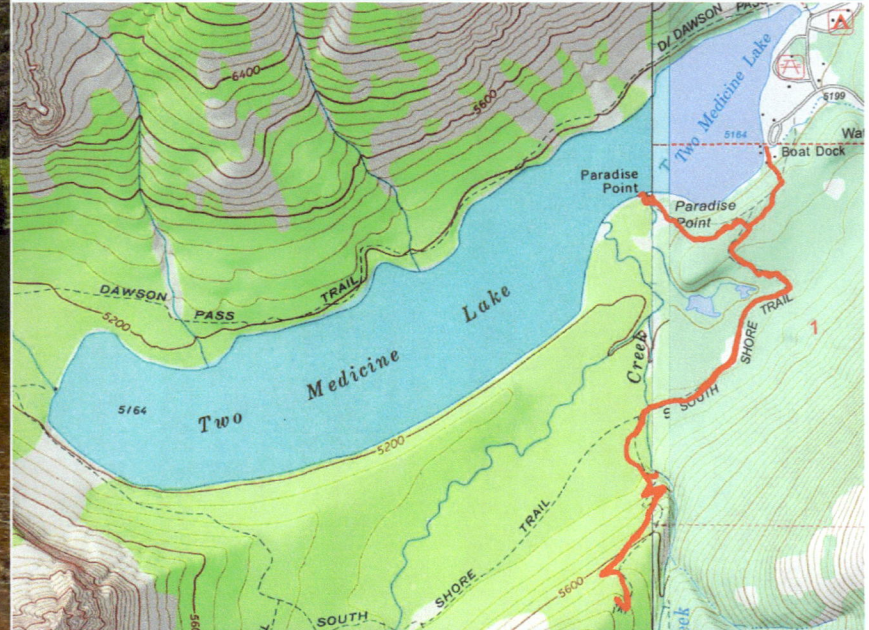

Approximate GPS data:
4.6 mile OB
750 ft ascend
2 hours

Pitamakan Pass & Dawson Pass Loop

Overview: 18 mile loop. Trails and TH are well marked. Head north along the short path that follows the shore of Pray Lake, cross the foot bridge and in a short distance you come to a marked trail intersection. For Counter clockwise loop, go right towards Pitamakan Pass. At a little over 6 miles you come to left branch for Oldman Lake, then it starts climbing up with switchbacks to Pitamakan Pass. Continue looping towards Dawson Pass for several miles that are fairly exposed along the Continental Divide with epic views. Descend down from Dawson Pass towards Two Medicine Lake with the last 3 miles along the lake easy and largely flat to rolling.

- Awesome hike and views! A favorite of mine. Loop either way, but counter clockwise the climbing has a little easier grades. Recommend trekking poles.
- Bring your camera and pick a fair weather day for the views: 360° panoramic views between the passes, Oldman Lake, Pitamakan Lake, No Name Lake and Two Medicine Lake.
- Two Medicine area is frequently windy. It can be cool and breezy on the passes. Consider hooded jacket, warm hat and gloves.
- Great for fall colors, and plenty of flowers June-July.
- Keep an eye out for moose and bears.
- Trail in excellent shape. Steep and narrow in spots.
- Take plenty of nutrition and water to cover this distance.
- You can save about 2 miles if you take the Two Medicine Lake shuttle boat back along Two Medicine Lake. Check for scheduling and tickets: glacierparkboats.com

Getting to the TH: Take Hwy 2 heading to East Glacier. Then take left heading north on MT-49. After about 4 miles, take a marked left on Two Medicine road heading to the park entrance and Two Medicine Lake. As you approach the Lake, take the first paved right at corner with Ranger Station towards day use and campsites. Continue through campsites until reaching day use parking slots on the Northeast side of Pray Lake for the North Shore TH. Bathrooms are near by.

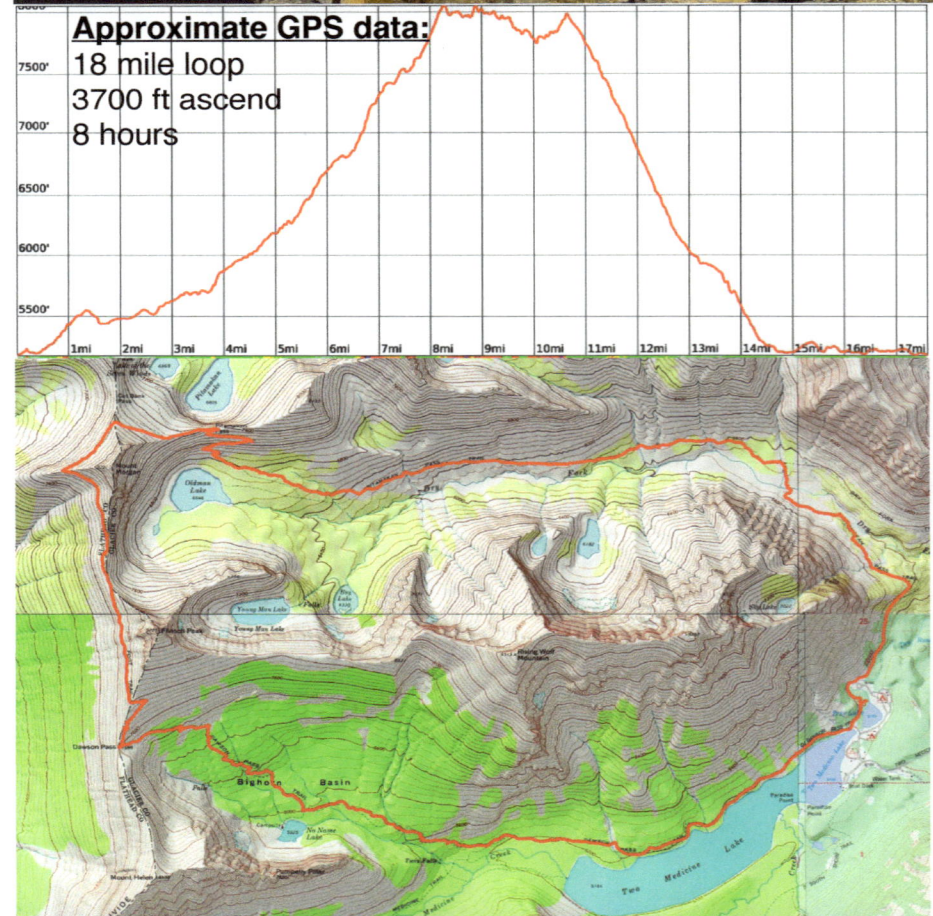

Approximate GPS data:
18 mile loop
3700 ft ascend
8 hours

Pitamakan Pass & Oldman Lake

Overview: 15.8 mile OB. Trails and TH are well marked. Head north along the short path that follows the shore of Pray Lake, cross the foot bridge and in a short distance you come to a marked trail intersection. Go right towards Pitamakan Pass. At a little over 6 miles you come to left branch for Oldman Lake, then it starts climbing up with switchbacks to Pitamakan Pass.

- Nice views from pass and of Oldman & Pitamakan Lakes.
- Two Medicine area is frequently windy and cool at the pass. Consider hooded jacket, warm hat and gloves.
- Great for fall colors, and plenty of flowers June-July.
- Trail in excellent shape.

Getting to the TH: Take Hwy 2 heading to East Glacier. Then take left heading north on MT-49. After about 4 miles, take a marked left on Two Medicine road heading to the park entrance and Two Medicine Lake. As you approach the Lake, take the first paved right at corner with Ranger Station towards day use and campsites. Continue through campsites until reaching day use parking slots on the Northeast side of Pray Lake for the North Shore TH. Bathrooms are near by.

Approximate GPS data:
15.8 mile OB
2600 ft ascend
6.5 hours

Running Eagle Falls

Overview: 0.6 mile OB.
- Easy/short hike that is basically flat.
- Nice view of Running Eagle Falls. Early season will be more spectacular with more water flow.
- Trail includes nature loop with interesting posted information.
- Trail in excellent shape.

Getting to the TH: Take Hwy 2 heading to East Glacier. Then take left heading north on MT-49. After about 4 miles, take a marked left on Two Medicine road heading to the park entrance and Two Medicine Lake. After the park entrance, but before getting to Two Medicine Lake is a right side pull out for this TH and has bathrooms.

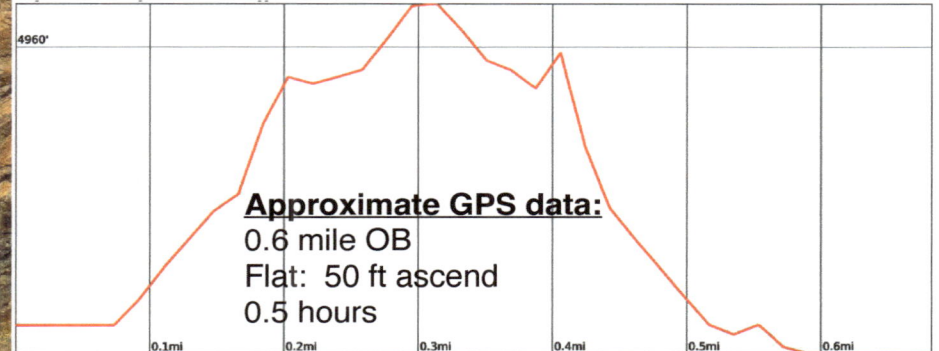

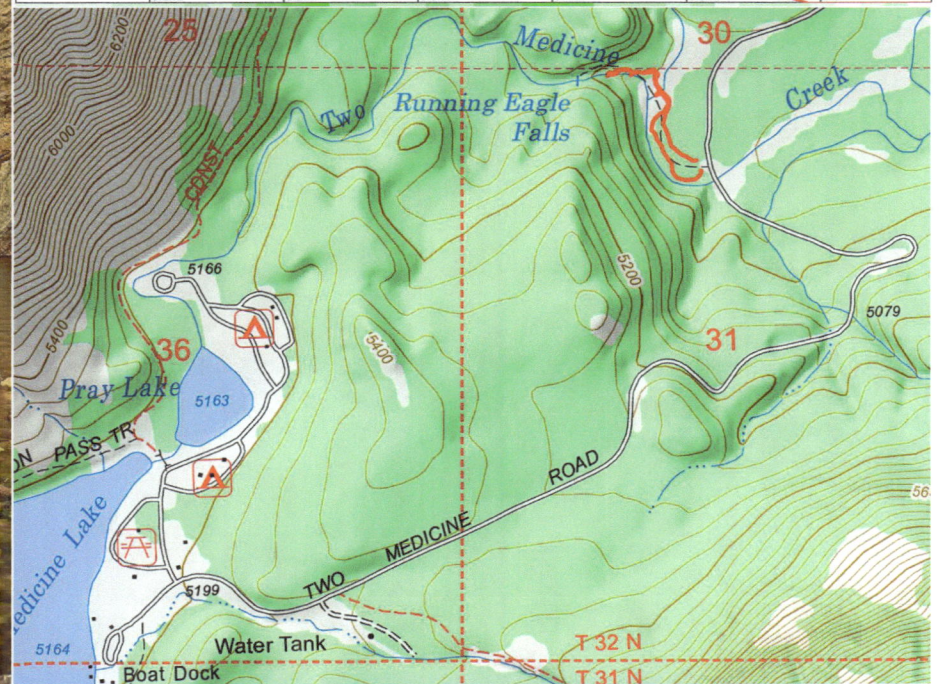

Approximate GPS data:
0.6 mile OB
Flat: 50 ft ascend
0.5 hours

Scenic Point

Overview: 8 mile OB. As you approach the 4 mile mark there is marked left branch to the Scenic Point overlook.

- Nice views of Two Medicine.
- Two Medicine area is frequently windy. It can be cool and breezy up high. Consider hooded jacket, warm hat and gloves.
- Keep an eye out for wildlife. You may see bears, marmots and bighorn sheep.
- The grades climbing are steady and not too bad. Trail in excellent shape.

Getting to the TH: Take Hwy 2 heading to East Glacier. Then take left heading north on MT-49. After about 4 miles, take a marked left on Two Medicine road heading to the park entrance and Two Medicine Lake. As you descend and approach Two Medicine Lake, take a left into the marked dirt TH parking lot.

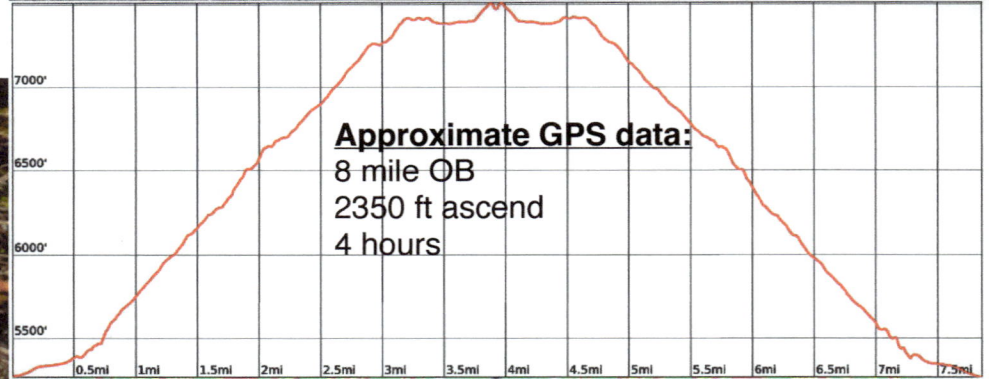

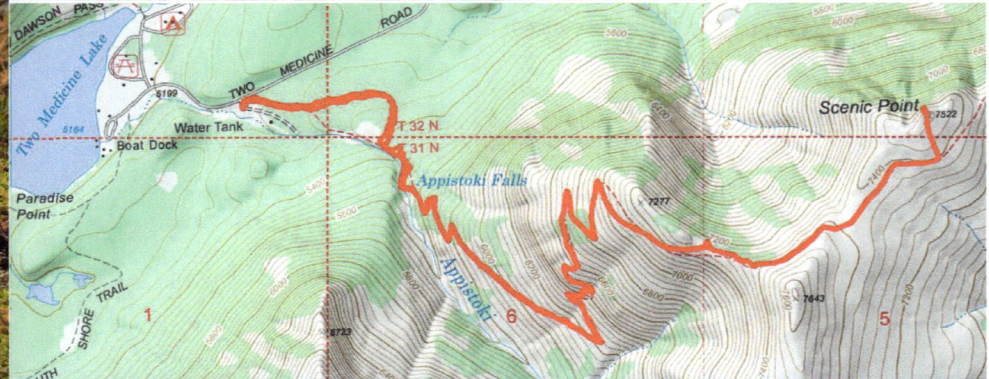

Approximate GPS data:
8 mile OB
2350 ft ascend
4 hours

Two Medicine Pass - Chief Lodgepole Peak

Overview: 16.5 mile OB. Start on the South Shore Trail near the Two Medicine Lake boat ramp area. This trail continues to Cobalt Lake and Two Medicine Pass. Rockwell falls view point is right off this trail. Trails and TH are well marked.

- Awesome 360° views on route to pass and Chief Lodgepole Peak along the Continental Divide. View of Cobalt lake from above. You can also see Mount Saint Nicholas and Lake Isabel.
- Keep an eye out for moose and bear on this trail.
- Trail in excellent shape. Easy going first few miles, and steeper as you climb to Cobalt Lake and to Chief Lodgepole Peak.
- Two Medicine area is frequently windy. It can be cool and breezy on the pass. Consider hooded jacket, warm hat and gloves.
- Take plenty of nutrition and water to cover this distance.

Getting to the TH: Take Hwy 2 heading to East Glacier. Then take left heading north on MT-49. After about 4 miles, take a marked left on Two Medicine road heading to the park entrance and Two Medicine Lake. Stay left as you approach Two Medicine Lake and park near the boat ramp and dock. The marked South Shore TH starts on the left side of the dock near the shoreline. Bathrooms are near by.

Approximate GPS data:
16.5 mile OB
2700 ft ascend
7 hours

Upper Two Medicine Lake & Twin Falls

Overview: 9.9 mile OB. Trails and TH are well marked. Head north along the short path that follows the shore of Pray Lake, cross the foot bridge and in a short distance you come to a marked trail intersection. Go left towards Upper Two Medicine Lake. The first 3 miles along Two Medicine Lake are mostly flat and easy.

- Nice views of Upper Two Medicine Lake and Twin Falls.
- Keep an eye out for moose and bears.
- Trail is in excellent shape. The climb to the upper lake starts at about mile 3, but the grades are not bad.
- Great for fall colors, and plenty of flowers June-July.
- Take the Two Medicine Lake shuttle boat both ways to shorten hike by approximately 5 miles. Check for scheduling and tickets: glacierparkboats.com

Getting to the TH: Take Hwy 2 heading to East Glacier. Then take left heading north on MT-49. After about 4 miles, take a marked left on Two Medicine road heading to the park entrance and Two Medicine Lake. As you approach the Lake, take the first paved right at corner with Ranger Station towards day use and campsites. Continue through campsites until reaching day use parking slots on the Northeast side of Pray Lake for the North Shore TH. Bathrooms are near by.

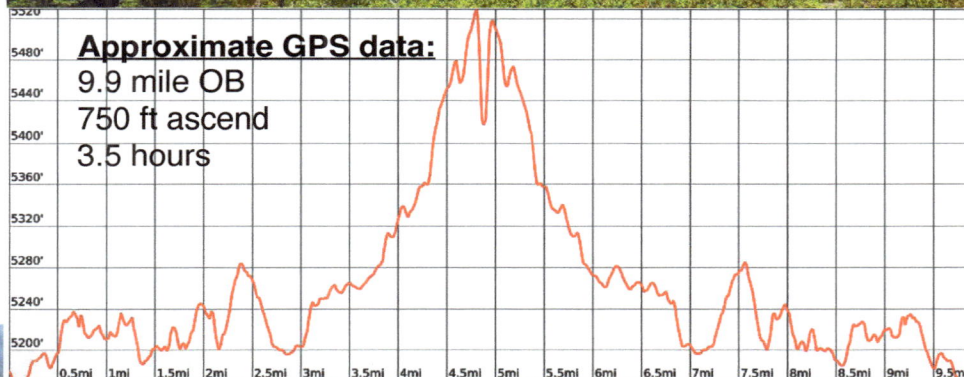

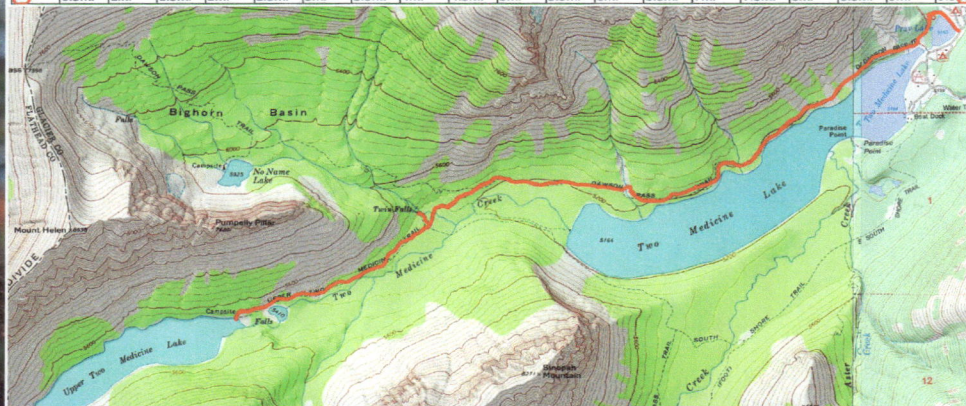

Approximate GPS data:
9.9 mile OB
750 ft ascend
3.5 hours

Glacier National Park - Many Glacier

Cracker Lake

Overview: 12.5 mile OB. Trails and TH are well marked. Stay left at first fork not far from TH. First 1.7 miles gets more horse traffic and can be muddy, chewed up and messy. After that the trail is in pretty good shape the rest of the way. Nicely shaded and more open as you approach the lake.

- Cracker Lake is very scenic with a beautiful turquoise color.
- Bring your camera.
- Keep an eye out for moose and bears on this hike.
- Recommend an early start to avoid getting behind a horse train.
- Not near as busy as some of the other trails in this area.

Getting to the TH: Head north on Hwy 89 towards Babb where you'll take a marked left for Many Glacier. Take a left towards Many Glacier Hotel as you approach Swiftcurrent Lake. Proceed past the hotel towards the upper parking lot. You will pass the marked trail head on the right at the south end of the parking lot as you enter it. There is a bathroom on the edge of the parking lot near the horse concessions.

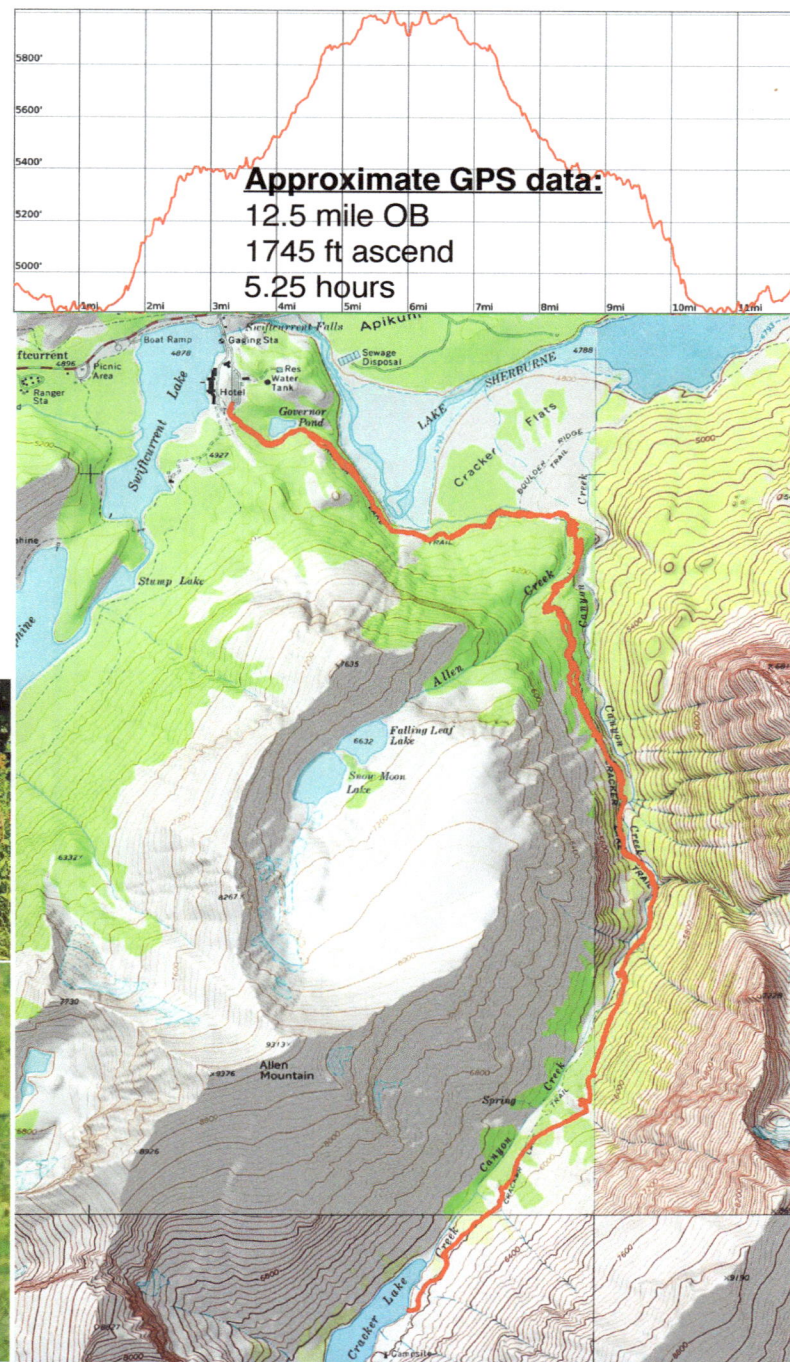

Approximate GPS data:
12.5 mile OB
1745 ft ascend
5.25 hours

Grinnell Glacier & Upper Grinnell Lake

Overview: 11.2 mile OB. The first 2 miles are flat and rolling along Swiftcurrent Lake and Lake Josephine. Then it starts to climb and you get views of Grinnell Lake below with Angel Wing in the background. There is a showering falls along the trail so bring a rain coat or poncho or get a little wet.

- This hike has awesome views including: Grinnell Glacier, The Salamander Glacier, Gem Glacier, Upper Grinnell Lake, Grinnell Lake, Lake Josephine, and Swiftcurrent Lake.
- Trail can have snow through June so check with the park for trail status.
- Trails are in great shape. Maybe a little overgrown on north shore of Lake Josephine.
- Trail can have plenty of flowers in the summer.
- You may see a variety of wildlife on this trail.
- This is a popular hike and trails can get busy.
- You can shorten the hike by a few miles using the shuttle boat options on Swiftcurrent Lake & Lake Josephine. Check for scheduling and tickets: glacierparkboats.com

Getting to the TH: Head north on Hwy 89 towards Babb where you'll take a marked left for Many Glacier. Continue straight towards Swiftcurrent Motor Inn when you come to the intersection for Many Glacier Hotel. After a short distance, take left turn into marked parking area for Grinnell Glacier TH. TH has bathrooms.

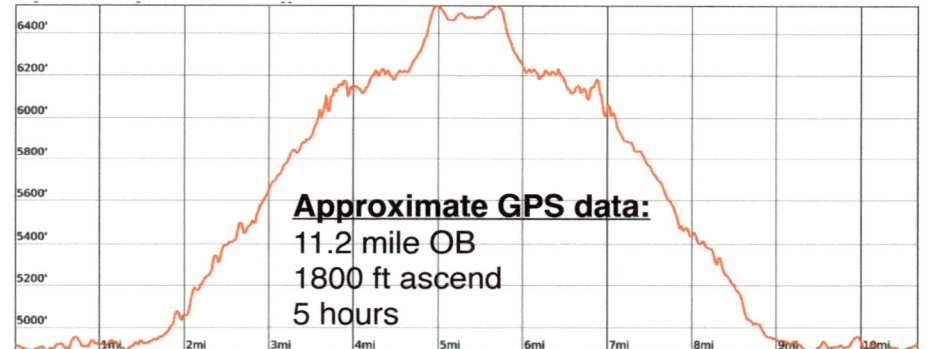

Approximate GPS data:
11.2 mile OB
1800 ft ascend
5 hours

Grinnell Lake & Lake Josephine

Overview: 8.1 mile OB/Loop. Trails are well marked and you can include trails on both the south and north shores of Lake Josephine. The views are a little better on the north shore of Lake Josephine.

- Nice views of Swiftcurrent Lake, Lake Josephine, and Grinnell Lake.
- Trails are in great shape. Maybe a little overgrown on north shore of Lake Josephine. Flat to rolling with easy grades.
- Trails can get busy.
- You can shorten the hike by about 5 miles using the shuttle boat options on Swiftcurrent Lake & Lake Josephine. Check for scheduling and tickets: glacierparkboats.com

Getting to the TH: Head north on Hwy 89 towards Babb where you'll take a marked left for Many Glacier. Take a left towards Many Glacier Hotel as you approach Swiftcurrent Lake. Proceed past the hotel towards the upper parking lot. The TH is on the south end of the hotel along the shore of Swiftcurrent Lake. There is a bathroom on the edge of the parking lot near the horse concessions.

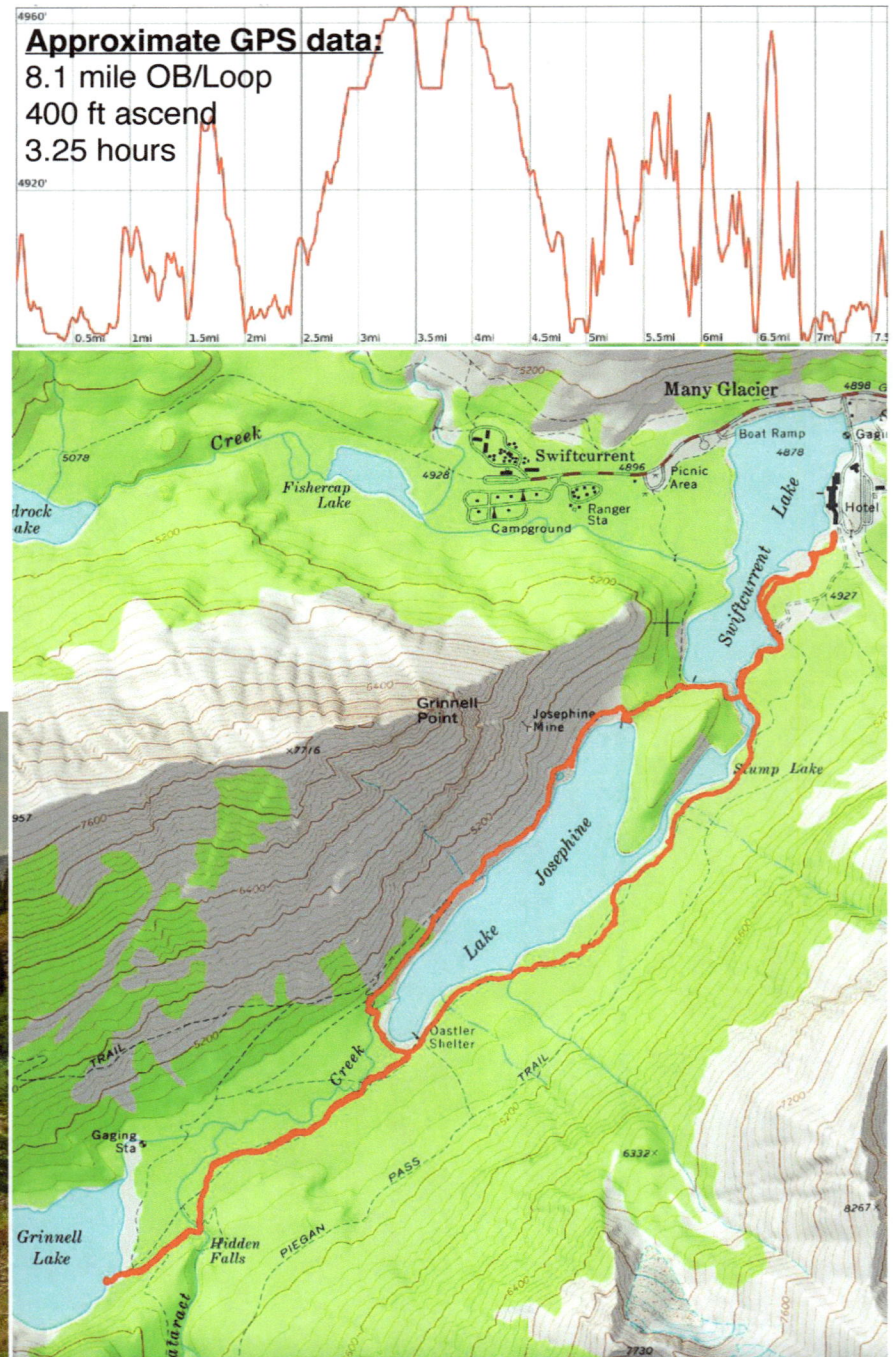

Approximate GPS data:
8.1 mile OB/Loop
400 ft ascend
3.25 hours

Iceberg Lake

Overview: 10 mile OB. Trail is well marked and has awesome views. Some shady sections but a lot of exposure which provides views for most the hike.

- Very scenic views of Iceberg Lake.
- Keep an eye out for moose along the trail. I came around a corner and was within 20 yards of a bull moose.
- Trail is very popular and can be quite busy. I recommend an earlier start.
- May still have snow near the lake in late June. Check with the park for current trail conditions.
- Plenty of flowers along the trail early-mid summer.

Getting to the TH: Head north on Hwy 89 towards Babb where you'll take a marked left for Many Glacier. Continue straight towards Swiftcurrent Motor Inn when you come to the intersection for Many Glacier Hotel. There are parking spots by the Swiftcurrent Motor Inn which I normally use and walk on the road that proceeds through some cabins to the TH. Bathrooms are near by.

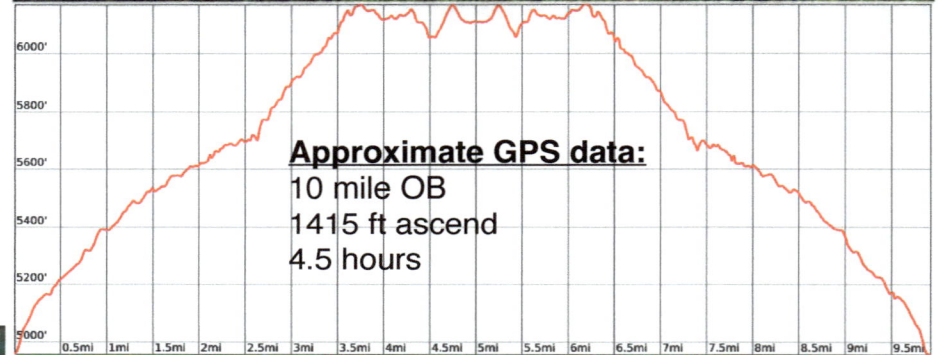

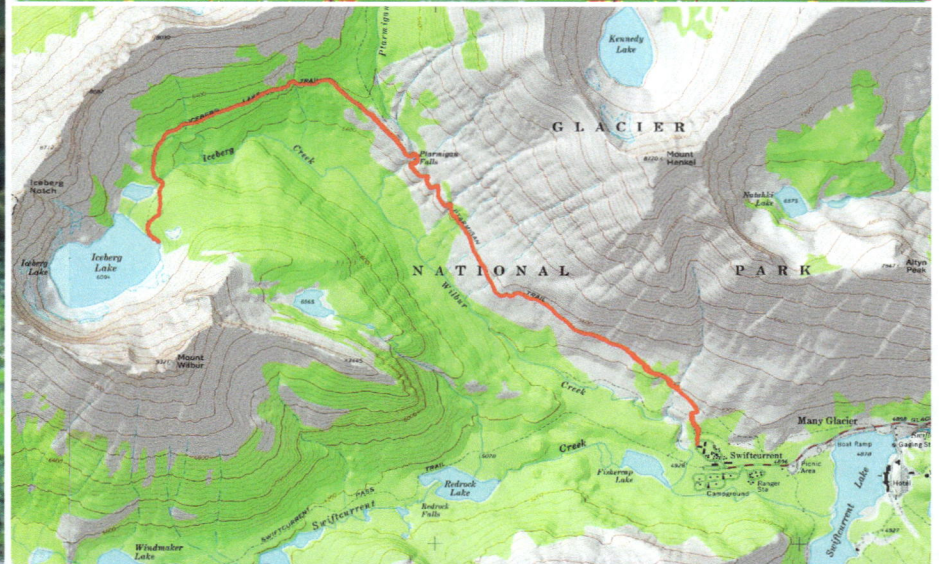

Approximate GPS data:
10 mile OB
1415 ft ascend
4.5 hours

Piegan Pass & Grinnell Lake

Overview: 18 mile OB (around 13 miles using the boat shuttles). I started from the Piegan Pass TH shared with Cracker Lake TH at the south end of the parking lot above the hotel…but I don't recommend this. The first 2.3 miles of this trail are fairly chewed up and messy from heavy horse traffic, and not so great views. I would recommend walking down the hill to the south end of the hotel and use the trail along the south shore of Swiftcurrent Lake and Lake Josephine. This trail is in much better shape and flat to rolling. As you near Grinnell Lake there is a left turn intersection for Piegan Pass. Grinnell Lake shoreline is not far from this intersection.

- This is a very scenic hike with awesome views from the pass, Swiftcurrent Lake, Lake Josephine, Grinnell Lake, and Morning Eagle Falls.
- Trails are in great shape and well marked. Again, my preference is to use the trail along the lakes (for both directions).
- Trail is busy to and from Grinnell Lake, but not to Piegan Pass.
- It can be quite windy on the pass. Consider packing a jacket with hood, a warm hat, and gloves.
- You can shorten the hike by about 5 miles using the shuttle boat options on Swiftcurrent Lake & Lake Josephine. Check for scheduling and tickets: glacierparkboats.com

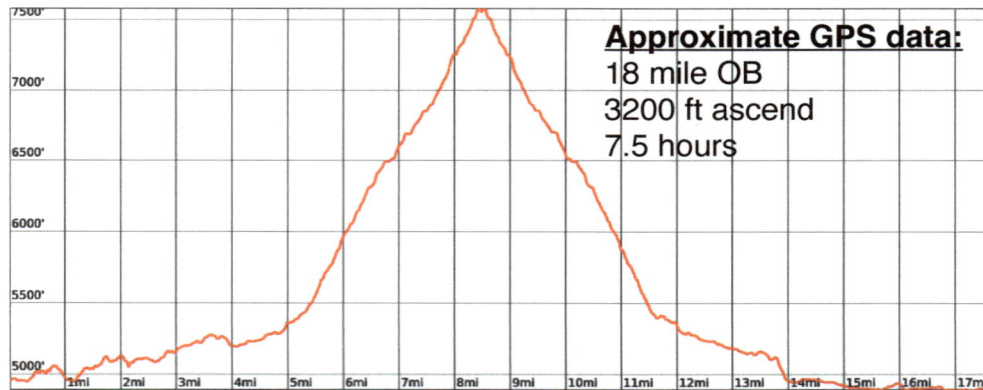

Getting to the TH: Head north on Hwy 89 towards Babb where you'll take a marked left for Many Glacier. Take a left towards Many Glacier Hotel as you approach Swiftcurrent Lake. Proceed past the hotel towards the upper parking lot. The TH is on the south end of the hotel along the shore of Swiftcurrent Lake. There is a bathroom on the edge of the parking lot near the horse concessions.

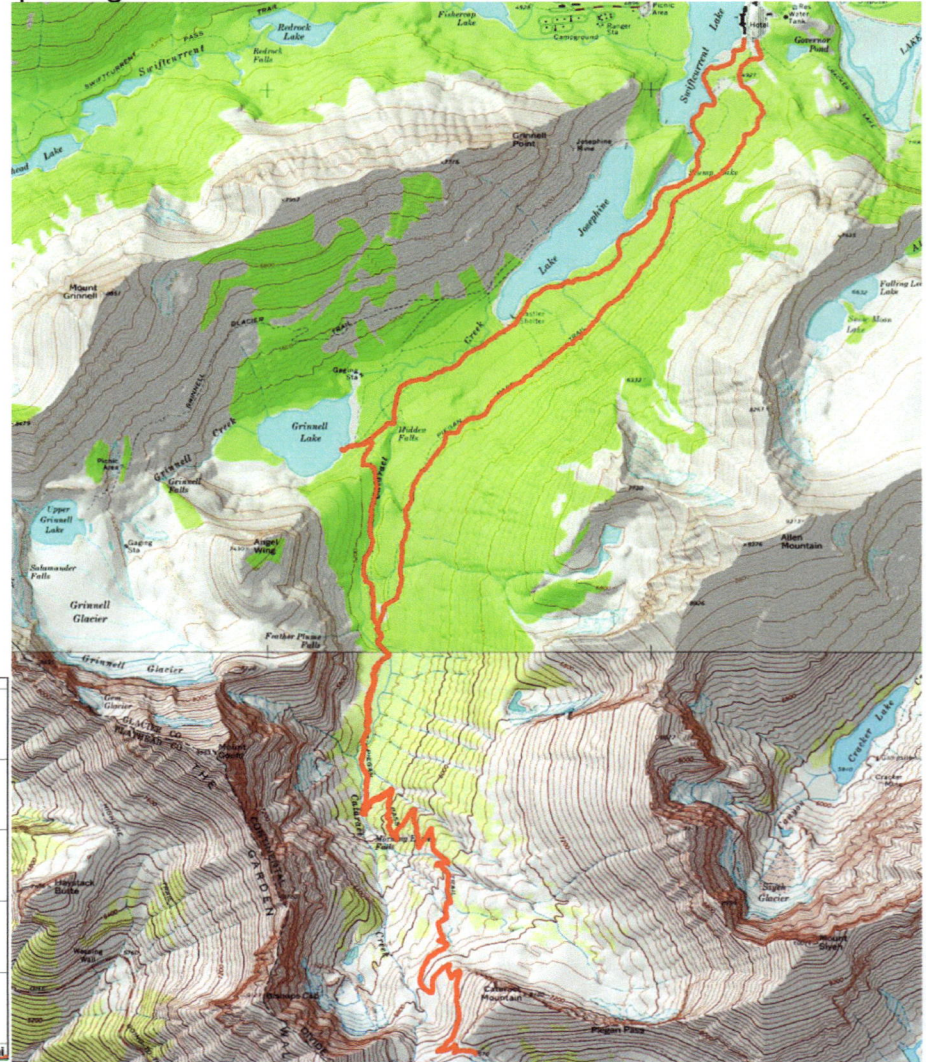

Approximate GPS data:
18 mile OB
3200 ft ascend
7.5 hours

Ptarmigan Tunnel

Overview: 10.8 mile OB. Trail is well marked and in great shape. At a little over 2.5 miles you come to a right fork for Ptarmigan Tunnel. You will start climbing steeper grades to Ptarmigan Lake and then to the Tunnel. Proceed through the tunnel for views of Lake Elizabeth, and descend down an extra 0.5 miles or so for views of Old Sun Glacier to the west.

- Very scenic views from both sides of the Tunnel.
- Keep an eye out for moose, bighorn sheep, mountain goats, and bears.
- This trail isn't near as busy as going to Iceberg Lake, but the first shared 2.5 miles or so can be busy.
- Plenty of exposure on this hike for the views.
- Check with the park for trail status early in the season (June) for snow conditions and if they have opened the tunnel doors.

Getting to the TH: Head north on Hwy 89 towards Babb where you'll take a marked left for Many Glacier. Continue straight towards Swiftcurrent Motor Inn when you come to the intersection for Many Glacier Hotel. There are parking spots by the Swiftcurrent Motor Inn which I normally use and walk on the road that proceeds through some cabins to the TH. Bathrooms are near by.

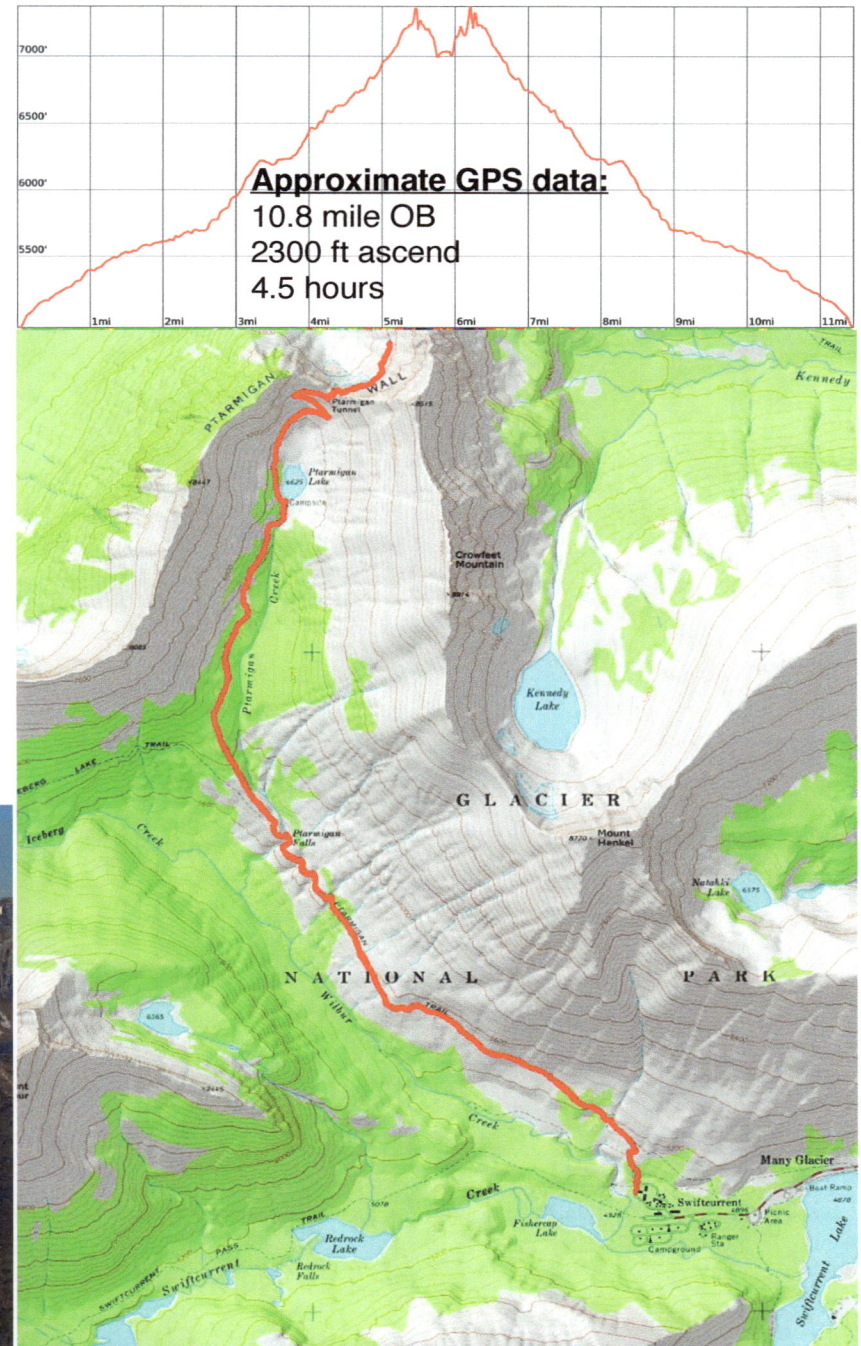

Approximate GPS data:
10.8 mile OB
2300 ft ascend
4.5 hours

Swiftcurrent Pass

Overview: 14.5 mile OB. Trail is well marked and in great shape. Not too much climbing the first 4 miles along the lakes. As you leave Bullhead Lake you start climbing with steeper grades to the pass.

- Awesome views climbing towards pass. Select a fair weather day for the views. It can be misty higher up towards the pass.
- Views of Swiftcurrent Glacier.
- Can be cool and windy on the pass. Consider packing a jacket with hood, a warm hat, and gloves.
- Keep an eye out for a variety of wildlife.
- Trail not as busy as some of the other hikes in Many Glacier.
- Check with the park for trail status and snow conditions. July through fall is best bet.

Getting to the TH: Head north on Hwy 89 towards Babb where you'll take a marked left for Many Glacier. Continue straight towards Swiftcurrent Motor Inn when you come to the intersection for Many Glacier Hotel. There are parking spots by the Swiftcurrent Motor Inn, and the TH is at the west end of the parking lot. Bathrooms are near by.

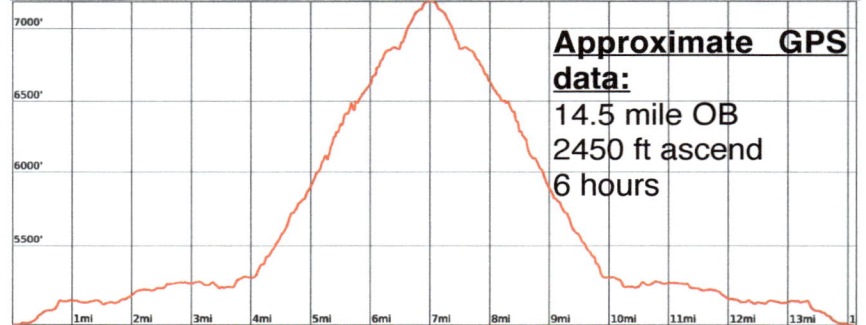

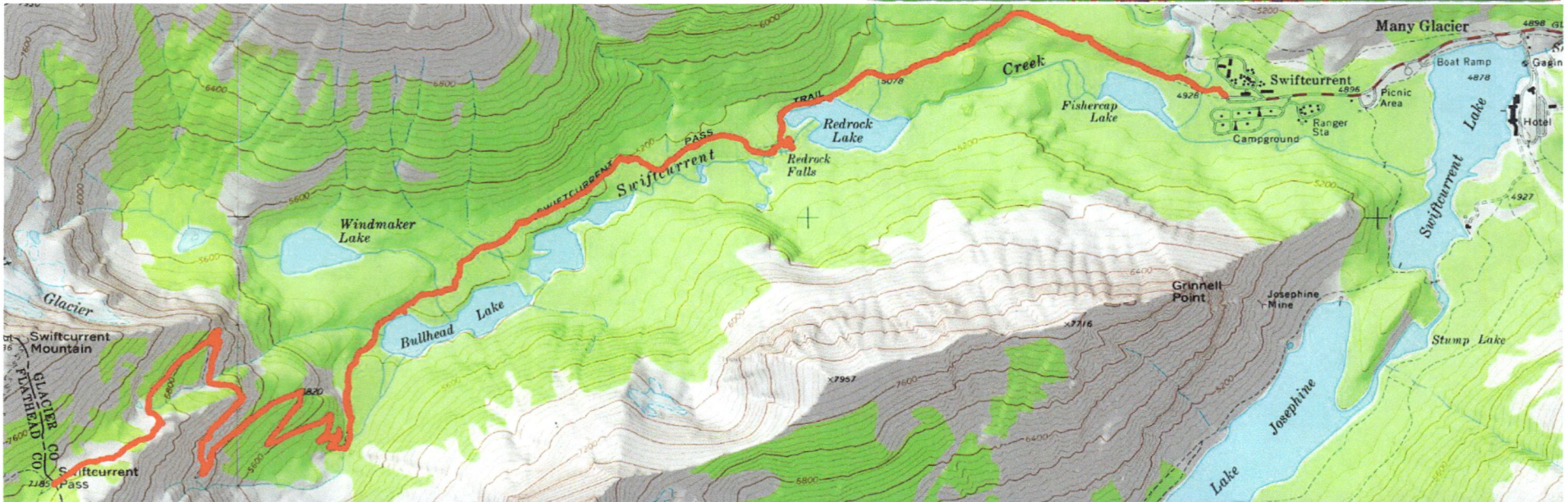

Approximate GPS data:
14.5 mile OB
2450 ft ascend
6 hours

Glacier National Park - North Fork

Glacier View Mountain

Overview: 4.5 mile OB. Just outside of GNP boundary. A little over 2 miles to the top and there are plenty of view points along the way for a rest. Fairly steep grade and a workout but worth the views and not a very long hike.

- Nice views of GNP, Huckleberry LO to south, North Fork Flathead River and even a glimpse of Flathead Lake to the south on the horizon (from top).
- Trail in pretty good shape. Steep in sections and loose rock so can slip especially coming down.
- Recommend trekking poles.
- Fairly exposed so likely hot on a warm sunny day. Recommend a cooler day.
- Recommend shoe spikes if early in the season with snow up higher.

Getting to the TH: Take Nucleus Ave to the north end of Columbia Falls, and turn right on North Fork Road (Hwy 486). Drive north for about 21.5 miles towards Polebridge. Just as you pass the right turn to West Glacier via Camas Road, park along right side of the road in wide pullout. The Demers Ridge Trail #266 begins across the road heading up the slope and is marked.

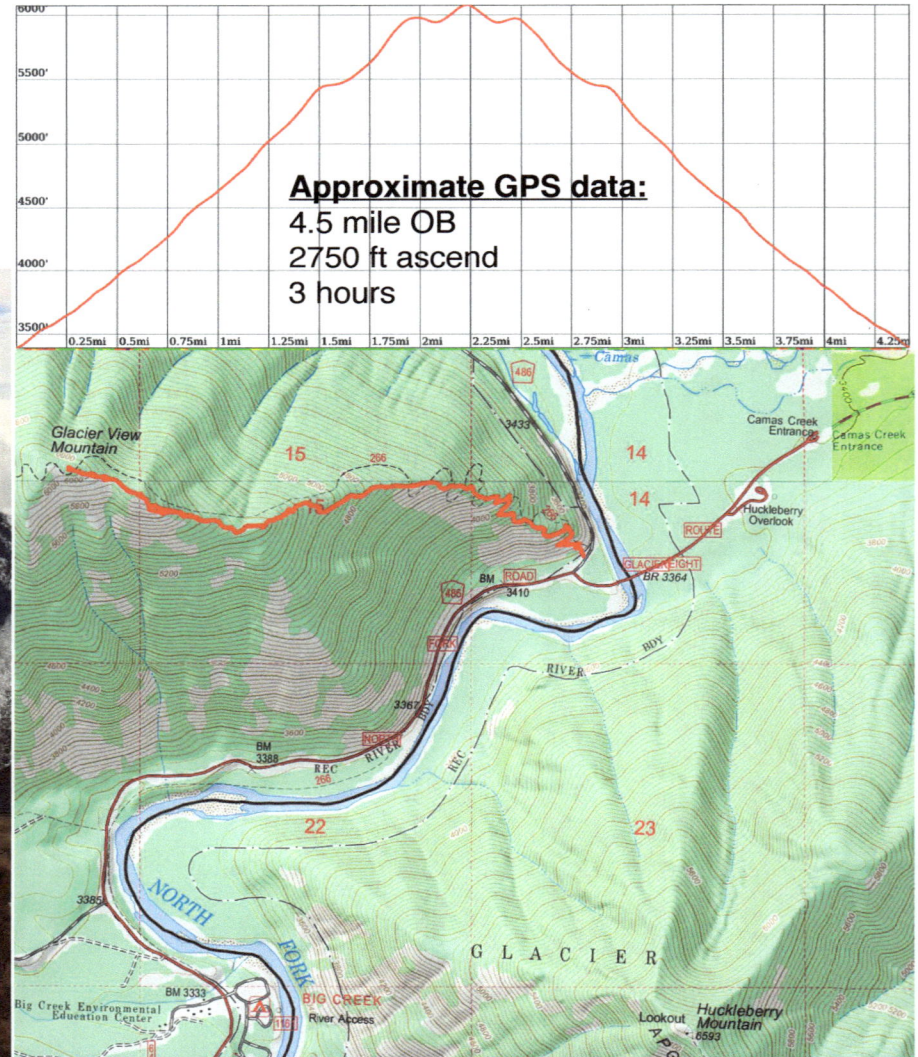

Approximate GPS data:
4.5 mile OB
2750 ft ascend
3 hours

Numa Ridge Lookout

Overview: 11.7 mile OB. Stay left from the day use parking area heading on the west side of Bowman Lake. You will come to a marked sign with mileage indicated. Continue on the west side of Bowman Lake for about 0.8 miles before the marked left fork for Numa Ridge Lookout. Once on the trail to Numa Ridge LO, it begins to climb at a fairly steady grade with an occasional break. The grade is not too bad.

- Nice views from the lookout.
- Trails are well marked and in great shape.
- The trail is largely in dense forest down below, and has more open sections as you get higher.
- Noted a few mosquitoes in June. If you hike in the fall, the Larch trees have nice colors and there are fewer bugs.
- Can be cool and windy up higher.
- Trail can be busy along Bowman Lake, but not to the lookout.

Getting to the TH: Take Nucleus Ave to the north end of Columbia Falls, and turn right on N. Fork Road (Hwy 486). Drive north for about 35 miles to Polebridge with much of it on gravel and can be dusty with washboard sections. Drive by the Polebridge Mercantile store and follow the signs to Glacier Park Entrance and Bowman Lake. It is another 6-7 miles to the Bowman Lake day use parking area and these roads are especially rocky and bumpy with narrow sections. Go slow. I would plan about 1.5 hours to drive from Columbia Falls to Bowman Lake. There are bathrooms in the day use parking area.

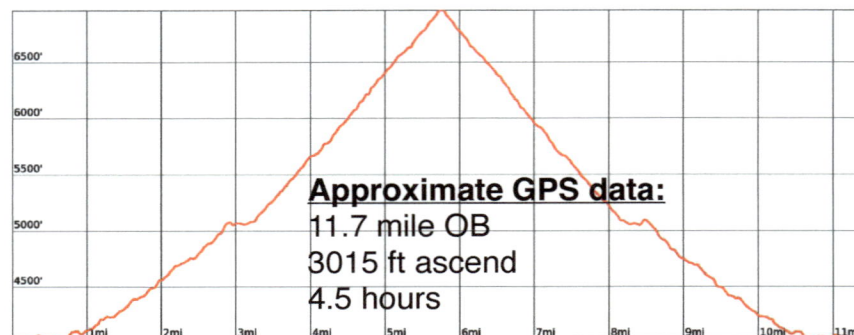

Approximate GPS data:
11.7 mile OB
3015 ft ascend
4.5 hours

Quartz Lake Loop

Overview: 13.25 mile loop. Stay right from the day use parking area heading on the east side of Bowman Lake. You will come to a marked sign with mileage indicated. I did the loop clockwise going to Quartz Lake and then to Middle Quartz, and finally to Lower Quartz Lake before heading back over the ridge to Bowman Lake.

- Trails are well marked and in good shape to Quartz Lake. Numerous trees down on the east side of the lakes and the trail was a little overgrown heading to Lower Quartz Lake.
- The trail is largely in dense forest with not many views except around the lakes. A lot of shade though.
- Very buggy.
- Grades not too bad except climbing up from Lower Quartz Lake it was steeper as well as descending down to Bowman Lake. A workout on that climb.
- Didn't see anyone else, but spotted a black bear in the parking area.

Getting to the TH: Take Nucleus Ave to the north end of Columbia Falls, and turn right on N. Fork Road (Hwy 486). Drive north for about 35 miles to Polebridge with much of it on gravel and can be dusty with washboard sections. Drive by the Polebridge Mercantile store and follow the signs to Glacier Park Entrance and Bowman Lake. It is another 6-7 miles to the Bowman Lake day use parking area and these roads are especially rocky and bumpy with narrow sections. Go slow. I would plan about 1.5 hours to drive from Columbia Falls to Bowman Lake. There are bathrooms in the day use parking area.

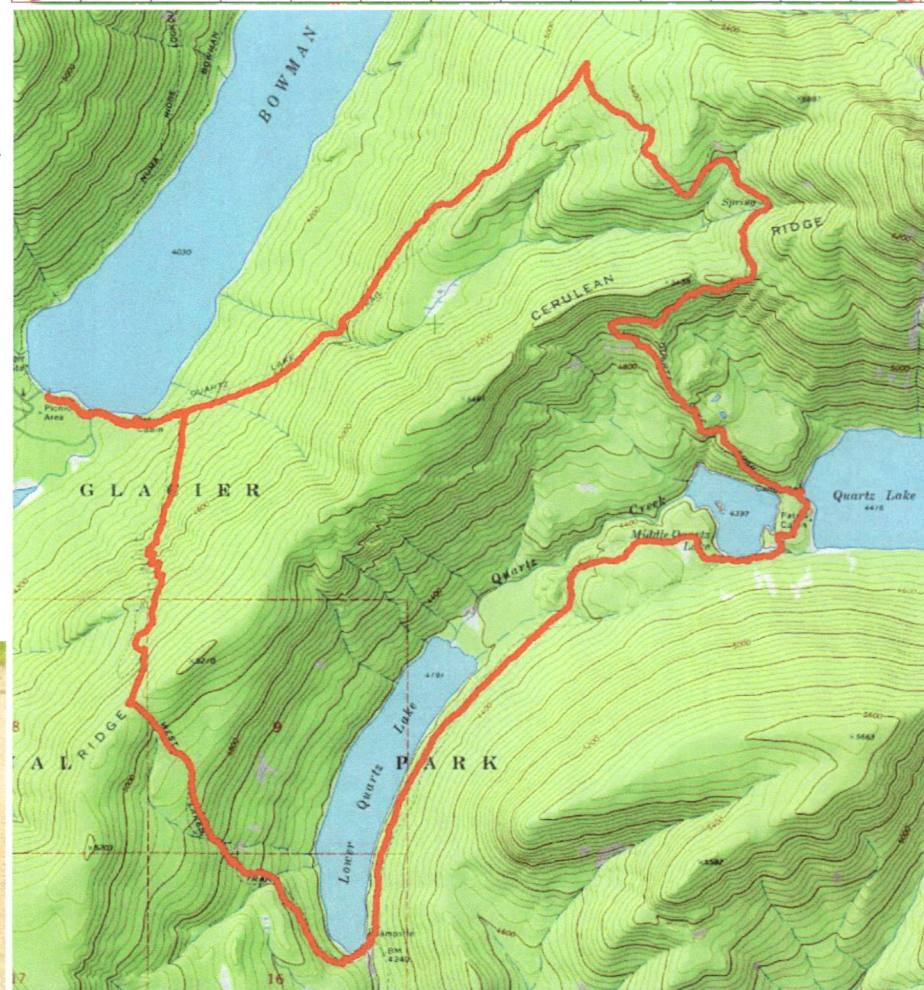

Approximate GPS data:
13.25 mile loop
2600 ft ascend
5 hours

Jewel Basin

Birch & Crater Lakes

Overview: 12.5 mile OB. Hike starts at the Camp Misery TH on trail #717. First 1.5 miles or so begins as a rocky rugged jeep path. Soon after you come to an intersection of many trails, look for signs on trees identifying trails. Take a right on trail #7 heading southeast for another 1.5 miles. Just before the view of Birch Lake will be a left fork on trail #724 to go around the east side of the lake for about 0.7 miles before hooking back up to trail #7. As you get to the south end of the lake look for signs on trees for trail #7. Take a left on trail #7 continuing southeast towards Crater Lake which you reach in a little over 6 miles total. Coming back just stay on trail #7 at Birch Lake to enjoy the views on the west side.

- Trails in great shape and marked. Look for signs on trees.
- Grades are not too bad since TH is fairly high up.
- Views of Flathead valley on route to Birch Lake.
- Both lakes are very scenic. One of my favorite Jewel Basin hikes.

Getting to the TH: Turn north at Echo Lake intersection off of Hwy 83 near Bigfork. Stay on paved road going past Echo lake and stay right at a fork keeping on a main paved road. Eventually stay right again on Jewel Basin Road which immediately goes to dirt. Stay on this dirt road until you get to Camp Misery TH and parking lot. The dirt road is pretty bumpy with wash boards, steep and narrow sections but 2 wheel drive can do it. Just drive slow in low gear and avoid the bumps as best you can. I think the road is an experiment on how bumpy a dirt road can get if no maintenance is done on it. Big TH and parking lot at Camp Misery with bathroom. Gets full and people park along the road too.

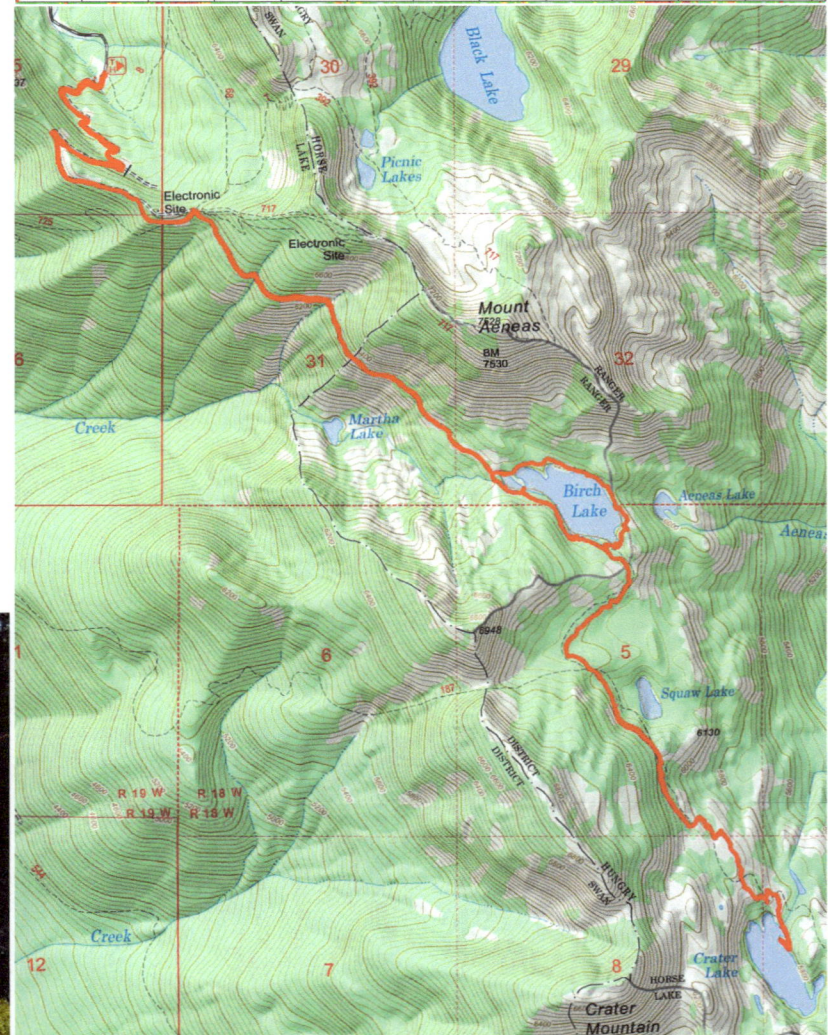

Approximate GPS data:
12.5 mile OB
1550 ft ascend
6.25 hours

Clayton Lake

Overview: 5.2 mile OB on Clayton Creek trail #420. Not as busy as other Jewell Basin hikes from the Camp Misery TH. Trail had overgrown brush in some spots and a number of fallen trees over the last mile approaching the lake.
- Plenty of wild flowers.
- Buggy especially at the lake if no wind.

Getting to the TH: Heading east on Hwy 2 through the town of Hungry Horse, turn right on the Hungry Horse Reservoir West Side Road. Cross the dam and continue to end of paved section and then on gravel until reaching marked right turn for Road 1633 with Jewel Basin Access. Continue on Road 1633 to TH parking lot.

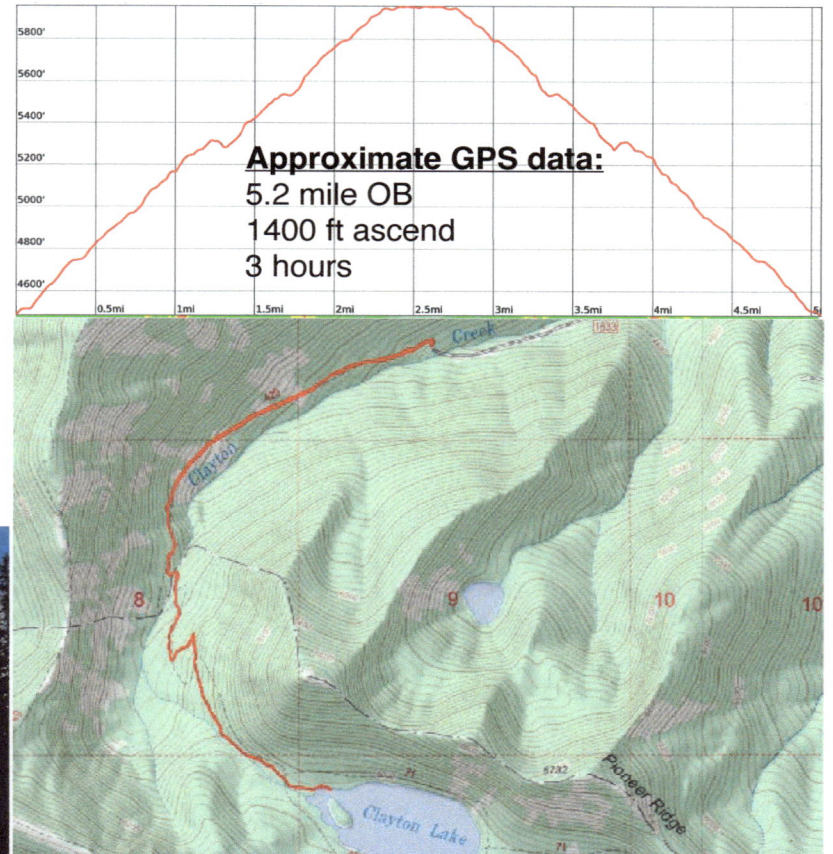

Approximate GPS data:
5.2 mile OB
1400 ft ascend
3 hours

Lake Loop: Twin, Blackfoot, Jewel Basin, Black, and Picnic Lakes

Overview: 11.3 mile clockwise loop (hike the other direction if you want).   Hike begins at the Camp Misery TH on trail #8 starting a clockwise loop. Stay left and continue past trail #68. Eventually trail #8 intersects with trail #7, go left on trail #7 towards Twin Lakes. Stay on trail #7 around Twin Lakes which offers nice views of the lakes. Next as you pass through some meadows you come to a right fork for trail #55 which you take heading towards Clayton Lake. After a short distance on trail #55 take right fork on trail #719 to Blackfoot Lake.   After passing Blackfoot Lake, continue climbing up on trail #719 towards Jewel Basin Lakes. After passing the first lake, take the right fork on trail #718 which will reconnect with trail #719 (go right when you reconnect). After leaving the Jewel Basin Lakes and a short distance on trail #719 you come to an intersection with Trail #1. Take a right onto trail #1 heading towards Black Lake. Continue on trail #1 past Black Lake (there is a left fork on trail #58 you can take down to the shoreline). After a short distance climbing up on trail #1, take the left fork on Trail #392 to Picnic Lakes. After the first Picnic Lake will be intersection with trail #717, stay right on trail #392 that continues around the first lake.   After a short climb you come to intersection with trail #7. Take a left on trail #7 which starts to descend down with switchbacks towards the TH. Eventually you come to a right turn on trail #68 heading back towards the TH. Trail #68 will intersect with trail #8 where you stay left and return to the TH parking lot.

- Trails in great shape and marked, but you do have to keep and eye out for the signs nailed to trees.
- Grades are not too bad since TH is fairly high up.
- Trail #719 by Blackfoot lake is a little overgrown in spots.
- Plenty of trail options to change it up, shorten, etc.
- Google Jewel Basin map PDF to download a trail map.

Getting to the TH: Turn north at Echo Lake intersection off of Hwy 83 near Bigfork. Stay on paved road going past Echo lake and stay right at a fork keeping on a main paved road. Eventually stay right again on Jewel Basin Road which immediately goes to dirt. Stay on this dirt road until you get to Camp Misery TH and parking lot. The dirt road is pretty bumpy with wash boards, steep and narrow sections but 2 wheel drive can do it. Just drive slow in low gear and avoid the bumps as best you can. I think the road is an experiment on how bumpy a dirt road can get if no maintenance is done on it. Big TH and parking lot at Camp Misery with bathroom. Gets full and people park along the road too. Go early to get a spot and avoid other cars on the dirt road (dust).

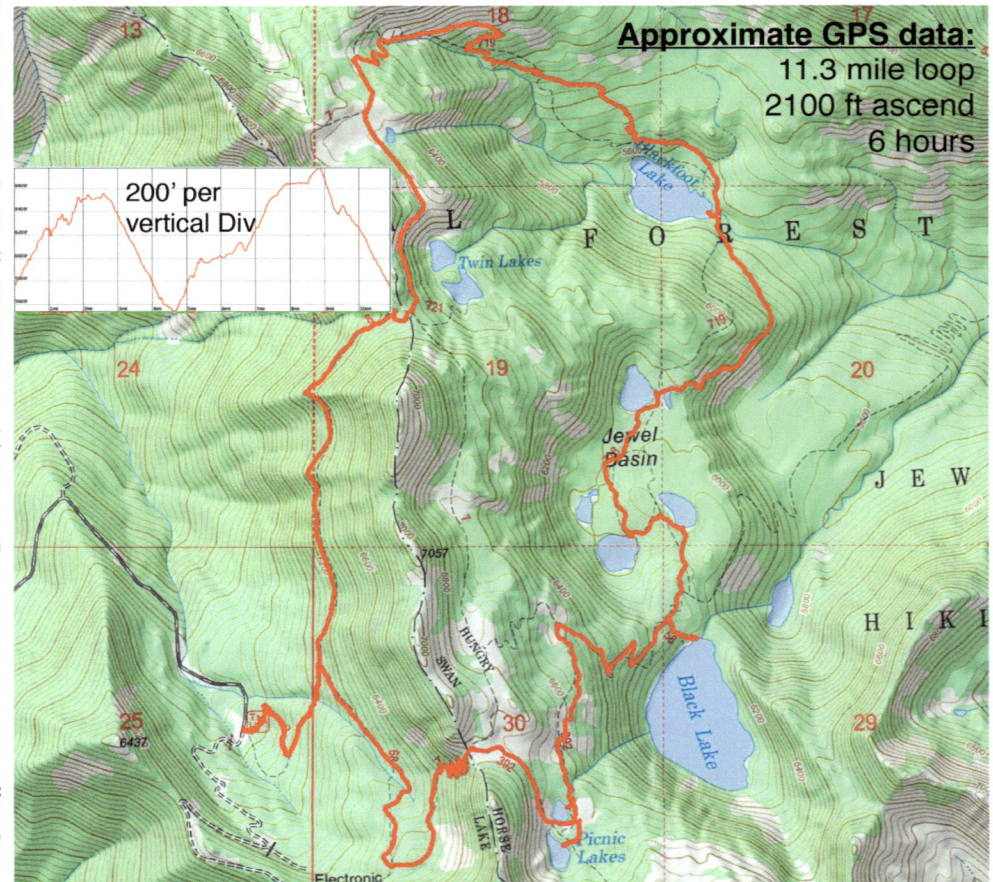

Approximate GPS data:
11.3 mile loop
2100 ft ascend
6 hours

200' per vertical Div

Mt Aeneas & Picnic Lakes Loop

Overview: 7 mile loop. Counter clockwise loop starts at the Camp Misery TH on trail #717. First 1.5 miles or so begins as a rocky rugged jeep path. Soon after you come to an intersection of many trails, look for signs identifying trails. Continue on trail #717 to Mt Aeneas and it starts climbing with steeper grades. You'll pass the microwave tower and continue up the ridge to Mt Aeneas. Nice views at the top. Trail continues down steep rocky ridge for a short distance before a sharp left which starts you looping back towards the Picnic Lakes. After descending to Picnic Lakes, take a left on trail #392 that runs between the two lakes. After a short climb, stay left on trail #7 heading back down to Camp Misery TH. Descend down steep switchbacks, and then take a right on trail #68 towards TH. Trail #68 eventually intersects with trail #8, take a left on trail #8 back to the TH.

- Nice views of Flathead Valley and towards Glacier National Park.
- May see Mt Goats on Mt Aeneas.
- Picnic Lakes are scenic.
- Trails in great shape and marked, but you do have to keep and eye out for the signs.
- Grades are not too bad the first 1.5 miles but are steeper climbing up to Mt Aeneas.

Getting to the TH: Turn north at Echo Lake intersection off of Hwy 83 near Bigfork. Stay on paved road going past Echo lake and stay right at a fork keeping on a main paved road. Eventually stay right again on Jewel Basin Road which immediately goes to dirt. Stay on this dirt road until you get to Camp Misery TH and parking lot. The dirt road is pretty bumpy with wash boards, steep and narrow sections but 2 wheel drive can do it. Just drive slow in low gear and avoid the bumps as best you can. I think the road is an experiment on how bumpy a dirt road can get if no maintenance is done on it. Big TH and parking lot at Camp Misery with bathroom. Gets full and people park along the road too.

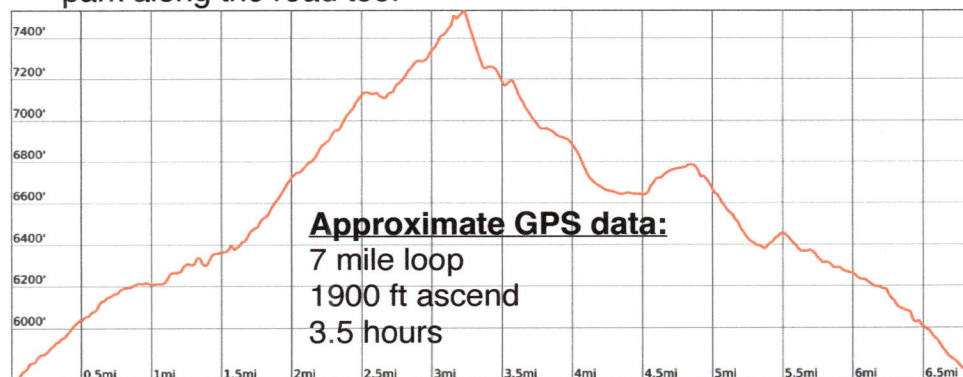

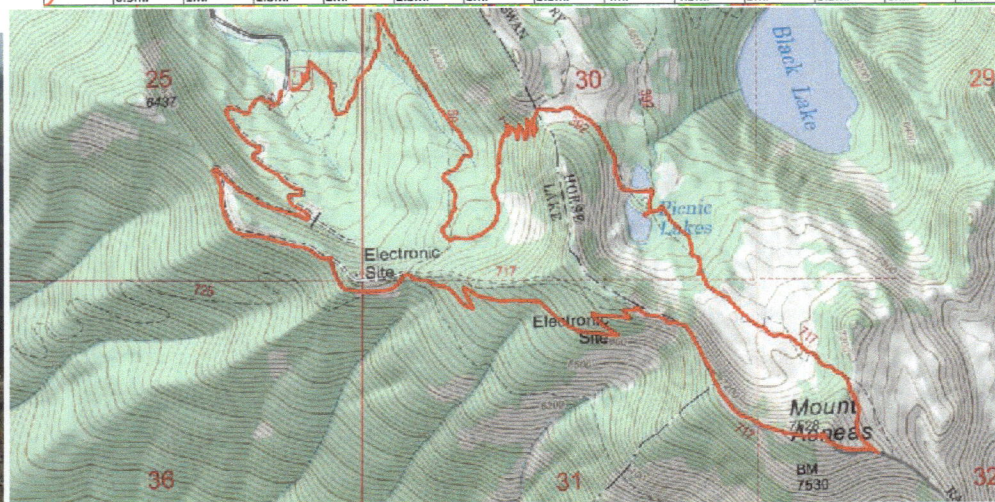

Approximate GPS data:
7 mile loop
1900 ft ascend
3.5 hours

Strawberry & Wildcat Lakes

Overview: 10.5 mile OB. Moderate grade with switchbacks climbing to Strawberry Lake. It flattens out for a section before the lake. Trail #7 intersects on the left and right before getting to Strawberry Lake shoreline. The sign post was knocked over and the trail on the right that heads to Wildcat Lake was overgrown and easy to miss. There is another overgrown trail 10-20 yards closer to the lake that hugs the shoreline…this is not the trail to Wildcat Lake. Take the overgrown right fork on Trail #7 to Wildcat Lake, it starts climbing up a slope with views of Strawberry Lake. The grades are steeper and a bit of a workout. Eventually the trail descends to Wildcat Lake.

- Nice views of lakes.
- Falls colors are awesome.
- Trail #7 is a bit overgrown leaving Strawberry Lake.
- Not as busy as hikes from the Camp Misery TH.

Getting to the TH: Turn north at Echo Lake intersection off of Hwy 83 near Bigfork. Stay on paved road going past Echo lake and stay right at a fork keeping on a main paved road. Stay left on paved Foothill Road when you go by Jewel Basin Road. Take a right on well marked dirt road 5390 to Strawberry TH (3 miles of decent dirt road to the TH).

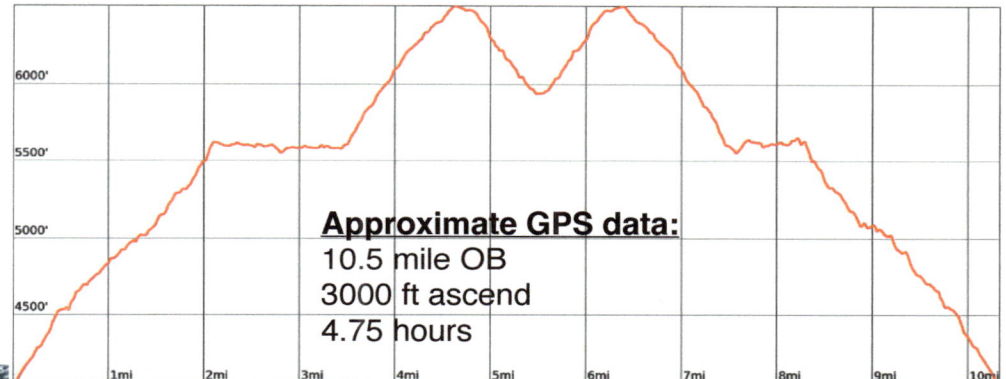

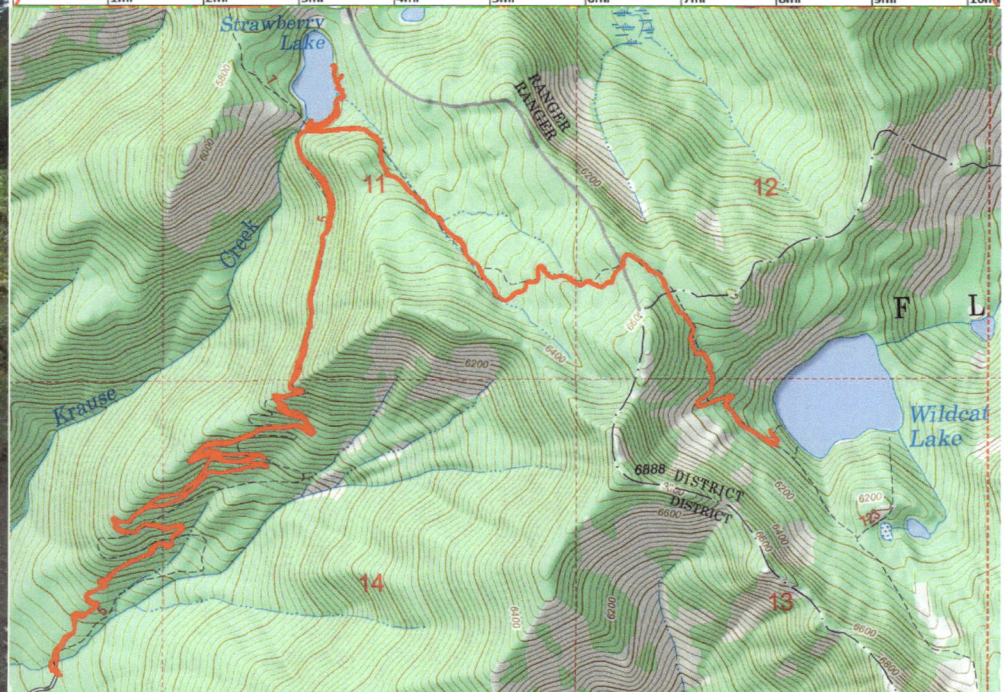

Approximate GPS data:
10.5 mile OB
3000 ft ascend
4.75 hours

Trail #7 overgrown, climbing up from Strawberry Lake to Wildcat Lake

Strawberry Lake Shore 10-20 yards

Strawberry Lake Trail

HWY 83 Swan Lake to Seeley Lake - Mission Mountains Wilderness

Cold Lakes

Overview: 5.9 mile OB. Trail to Lower Cold Lake is about 4 miles RT and in good shape. An extra mile to Upper Cold Lake which in my opinion is a little more scenic and worth it. The trail around the lower lake is a bit crude with fallen trees and brush and has a few options to pick from. Once you get to the end of the lake there is a stretch of uphill before getting to the upper lake.

- Crude trail, overgrown and down trees around the lower lake.
- Some bugs.
- Trail maybe wet in spots and offers good shade.

Getting to the TH: South of Swan Lake on Hwy 83 and just north of the Mission Mountain Mercantile between mile markers 46 and 47. Look for the Cold Lakes sign on Hwy 83. About 7 miles of dirt roads to the TH which are marked and in good shape (dirt roads: 903, 9568, 9599). TH parking is fairly large and has a bathroom.

Approximate GPS data:
5.9 mile OB
850 ft ascend
2.75 hours

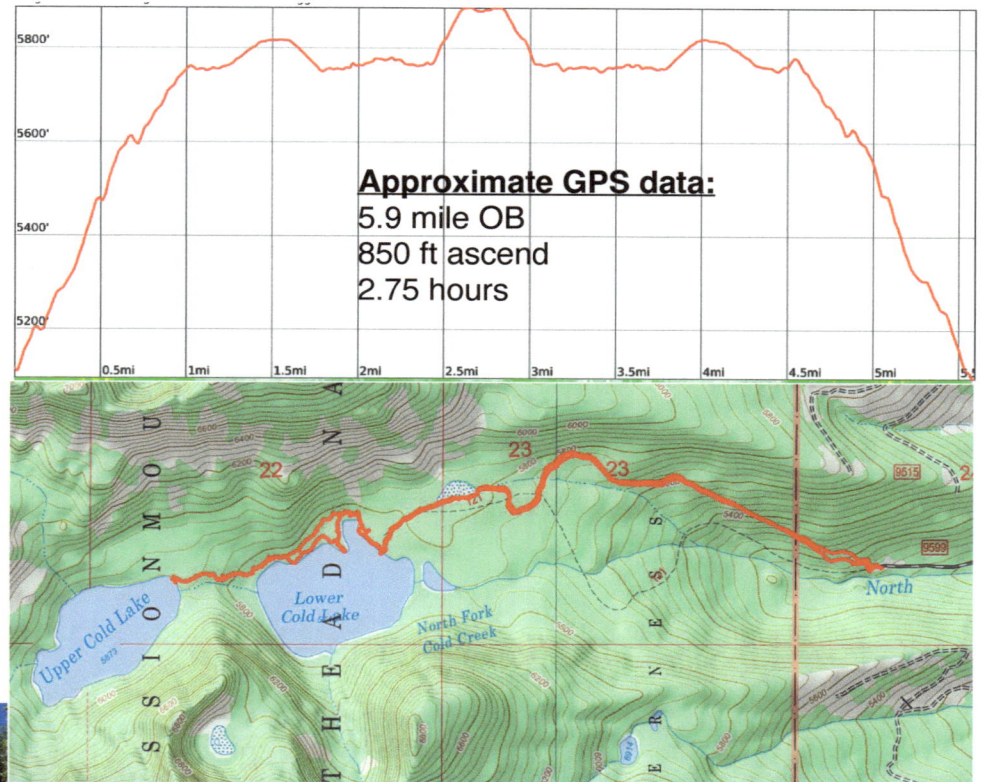

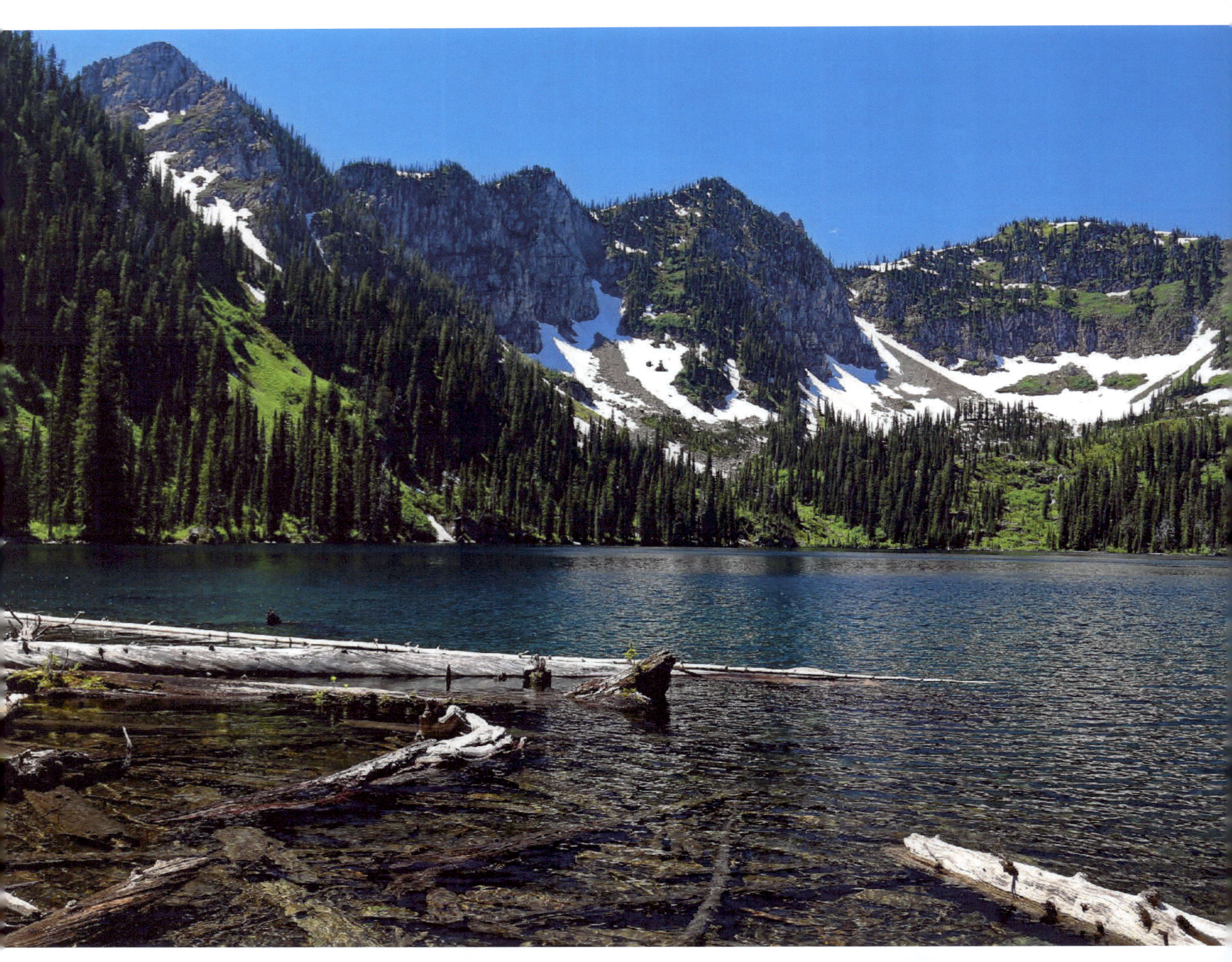

Crescent, Heart and Glacier Lakes

Overview: 9.3 mile OB. Hike to Crescent and Heart Lakes by staying right at first intersection at about 1 mile (left goes to Glacier Lake). At about 3 miles stay right to go to Crescent and Heart Lakes. Coming back you can add about 0.6 miles RT to go Glacier Lake at the fork about a mile from the TH.

- Trails in good shape and marked with signs.
- Grades are fairly easy.
- Descent shade on this hike.
- Scenic lakes and views.
- Can be busy on weekends. Start early to get parking.

Getting to the TH: South of Swan Lake and Condon on Hwy 83, take a right on Kraft Creek Road #561 between mile markers 38 and 37. About 11 miles of dirt road to nice TH with bathroom. Dirt road is good but has numerous washboard sections.

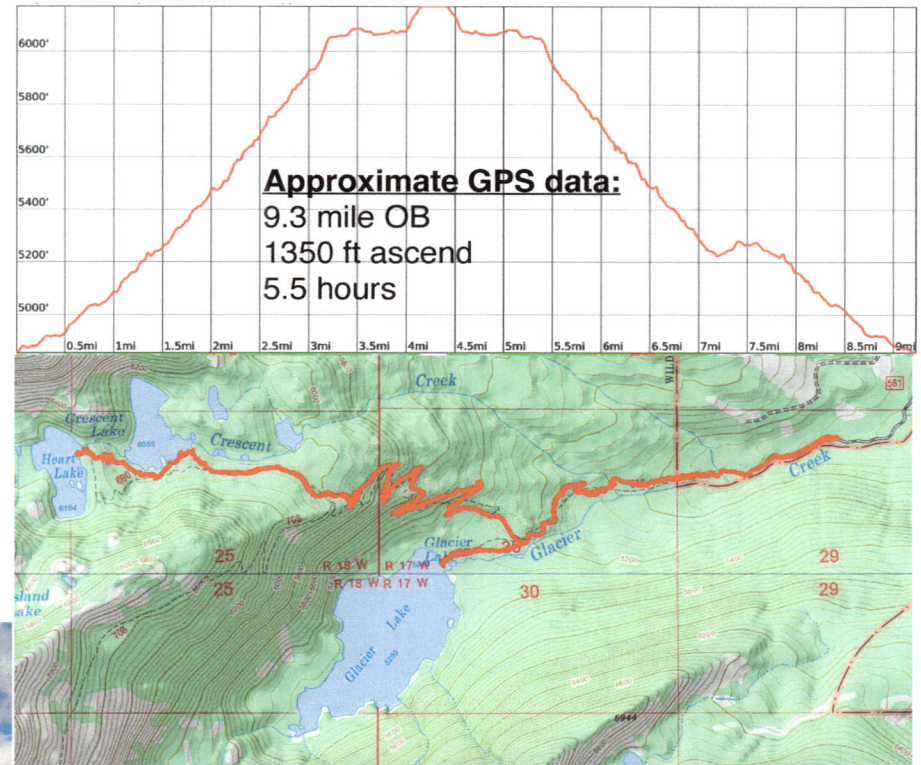

Approximate GPS data:
9.3 mile OB
1350 ft ascend
5.5 hours

Crystal Lake from North Trailhead

Overview: 5 mile OB. Hike begins from North TH on trail #351. At about 2 miles and after descending down towards the lake you come to a 4 way intersection. Trail #351 is marked and goes to both the North TH and the South TH. Trail #490 is marked and goes to the end of Lindbergh Lake. The unmarked trail heads west to Crystal Lake which is what we want, and in about 0.2 miles you will see the lake and shore.

- Trails in good shape. There are a lot of tree roots and rocks to navigate so trekking poles help.
- Didn't notice bugs but had some wind.
- Didn't see anyone and only car at the TH.
- Save your energy for the climb back to TH. Grade is not extreme but a good work out for about 1.75 miles.

Getting to the TH: South of Condon on Hwy 83, take the Lindbergh Lake Road #79. Continue on Road #79 towards the campground and boat access, stay right at major fork. Just before the campground and boat ramp take the right fork staying on Road #79 to Crystal Lake TH. From this fork about another 7 miles before the marked TH where Road #79 ends.

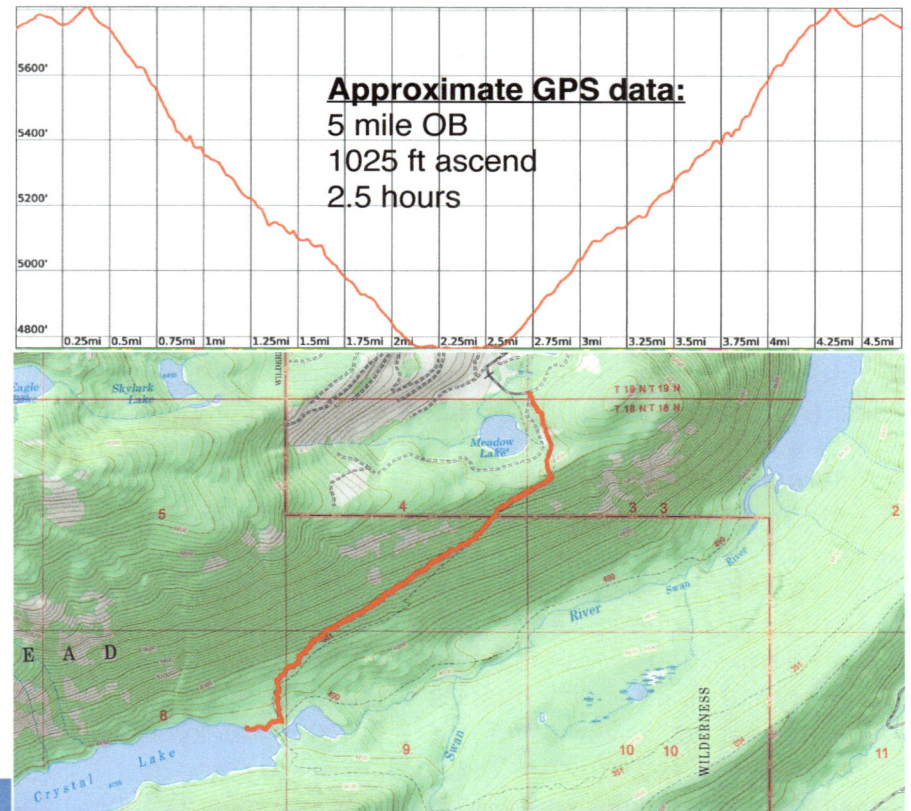

Approximate GPS data:
5 mile OB
1025 ft ascend
2.5 hours

Hemlock Lakes Loop

Overview: 12 mile loop. Clockwise loop starts from Hemlock Lake TH with trail #607. Go 3.3 miles on #607 to left fork on trail #695 for Hemlock Lake. It's 0.3 miles from the fork to Hemlock Lake. Return from Hemlock Lake to #607 intersection and take a left going 1.1 miles towards North Hemlock Lake and at about 5 miles total from TH come to an unmarked/faint intersection with trail #515. Take left on unmarked trail #515 for North Hemlock Lake and go about 1.3 miles to North Hemlock Lake. Return back from the lake 1.3 miles to intersection and this time continue loop by staying left or straight on trail #515. Continue on #515 for about 3.8 miles (trail becomes an old road approaching TH) to the Hemlock Peak TH sign and parking area. Stay right to complete the loop and hike another 0.5 miles on the road you drove in on to the upper parking area for Hemlock Lake TH.

- Lakes are scenic. Much of the trail is through old burn area with new growth and not too scenic. Plenty of sun exposure.
- Plenty of Huckleberry bushes along the way.
- Trail is a little overgrown in some spots, rocky, but pretty good overall. Grades on ridges pretty steady and not too bad for climbing. A little steeper on segments approaching the two lakes.
- Did not encounter any other hikers.

Getting to the TH: Take Hwy 83 south of mile marker 38, turn right on Kraft Creek Road #561. Go about 6.5 miles on Kraft Creek Road #561 to right fork on #9576 for Hemlock Lake TH and Hemlock Peak TH. Go a short distance to a bridge crossing and continue past a right hand parking area for the Hemlock Peak TH (Trail 515) which also goes to North Hemlock Lake. Go another 0.5 miles on rocky rough road with a short rutted section to the upper parking area for the Hemlock Lake TH #607. If you don't want to drive the rocky road section and still want to hike the clockwise loop, park at the first TH and walk up the road 0.5 miles and begin on the Hemlock Lake TH #607.

Approximate GPS data:
12 mile loop
2650 ft ascend
5 hours

Piper Lake & Ducharm Lake

Overview: 13.2 mile OB. Trail #119 begins on the opposite side of the road from the wood sign and small parking area. Hike 5.3 miles to the foot of Piper Lake, and 6 miles to the head of Piper Lake. Go an extra 0.6 miles to Ducharm Lake (after climbing up from Piper Lake a few tenths of a mile, take unmarked left fork on a crude/faint trail heading downhill to Ducharm Lake).

- Scenic lakes.
- Ducharm Lake was worth the extra distance.
- Hike largely in forest with plenty of shade. Open views mostly around the lakes.
- Trail in general was good, rolling with overall elevation gain. Grades are pretty easy. Gets steeper at about mile 4 as you head up to Piper Lake.
- Trail is a little overgrown in spots and has plenty of rocks and roots to navigate around and keep your attention.
- Not a busy hike and didn't see anyone.

Getting to the TH: Head south on Hwy 83 past mile marker 54, take marked right turn on dirt road 966 Piper Creek Rd. Go about 4.7 miles to TH. TH is just before a wood bridge stream crossing and has some left side parking with a large wood sign. Trail begins on opposite side of road across from sign and parking area.

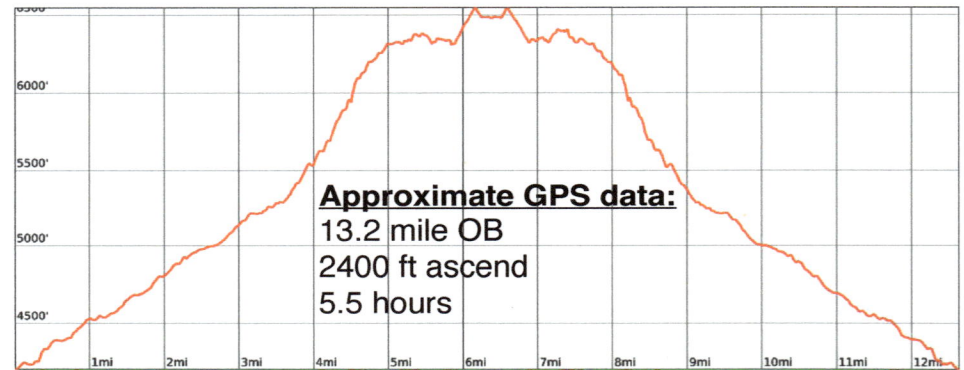

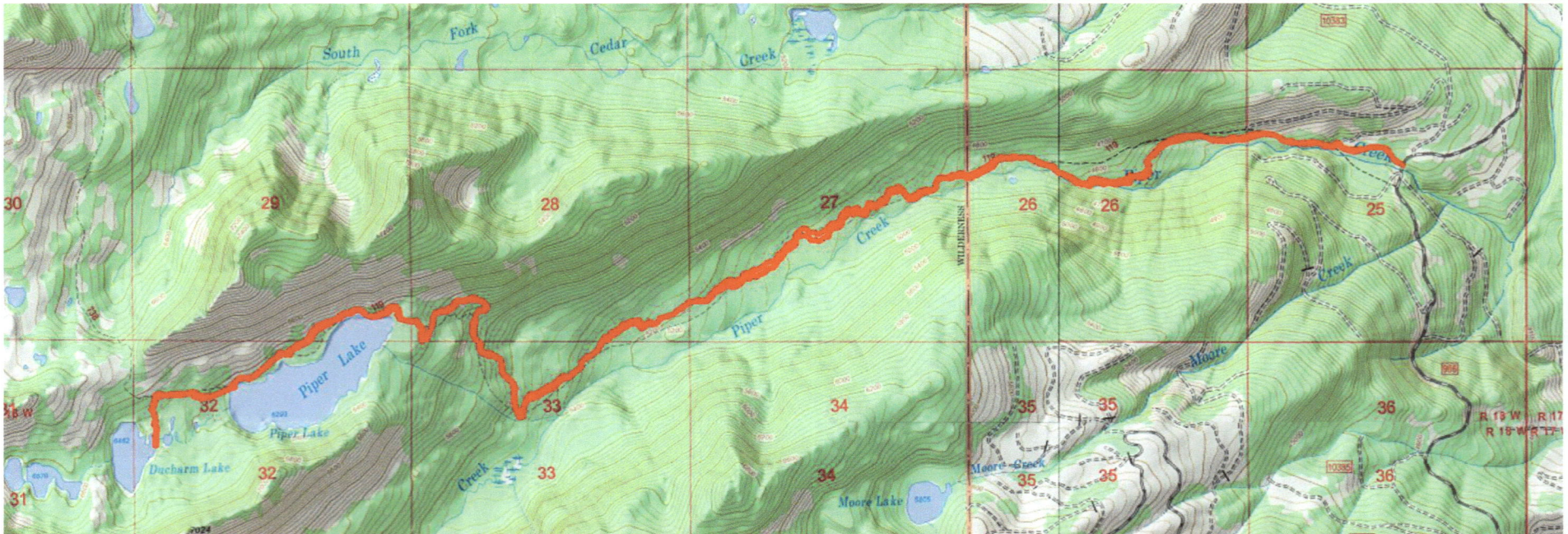

Approximate GPS data:
13.2 mile OB
2400 ft ascend
5.5 hours

Turquoise Lake

Overview: 12.8 mile OB. Stay right at first intersection at about 1 mile (left goes to Glacier Lake). At about 3 miles stay left to go to Turquoise Lake. As you get closer to the lake you navigate through rock slabs.

- Very scenic views of Turquoise Lake, Glacier Lake, and smaller lakes as you approach Turquoise Lake.
- Trails in good shape.
- Grades steady and not bad.
- Trail can be busy especially on weekends and gets backpackers and campers. Start early to get a parking spot.

Getting to the TH: South of Swan Lake and Condon on Hwy 83, take a right on Kraft Creek Road #561 between mile markers 38 and 37. About 11 miles of dirt road to nice TH with bathroom. Dirt road has numerous washboard sections.

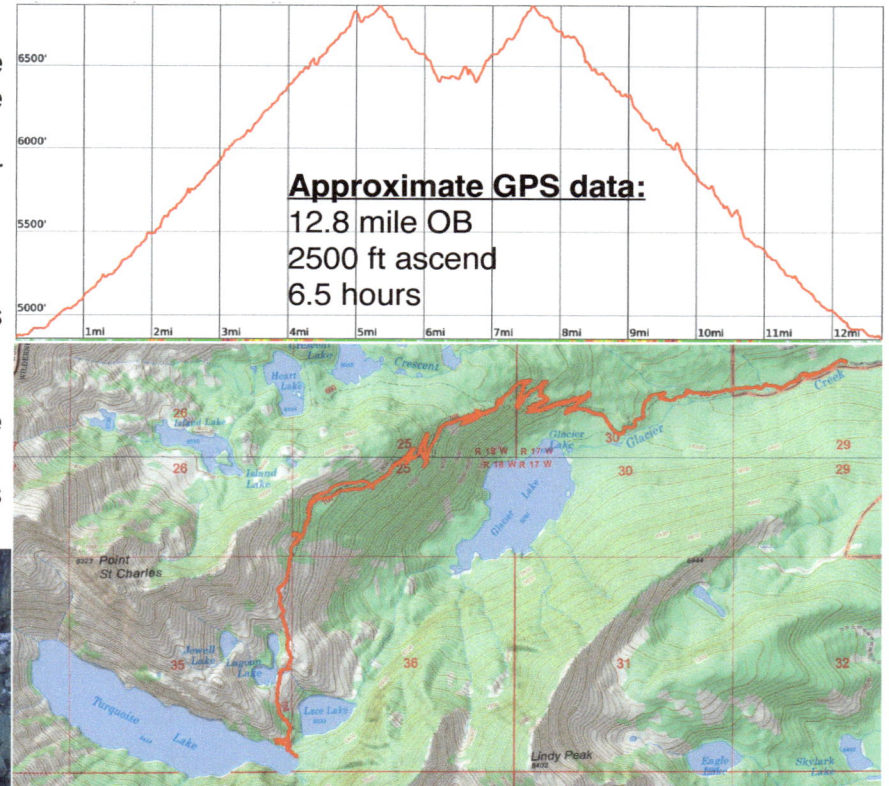

Approximate GPS data:
12.8 mile OB
2500 ft ascend
6.5 hours

HWY 83 Swan Lake to Seeley Lake - Swan Range

Hall Lake

Overview: 8.5 mile OB to foot of lake. Trail #61. 10.5 mile OB to Trail #7 intersection. Hike starts through a recent clear cut area for about 0.75 miles before entering the forest. At 1.3 miles had to remove shoes to wade across creek in June.

- Lake is scenic but has some brush around it.
- Campsite at the foot of the lake.
- May have to wade lake outlet stream or cross logs early in the season at the foot of the lake.
- Trail in pretty good shape with some fallen trees.
- Grades are not bad.
- Not busy and may not see anyone.
- Deep snow at Trail #7 may exist in June.

Getting to the TH: Heading south on Hwy 83 into the town of Swan Lake past mile marker 72, take a left at the Laughing Horse Lodge on Fenby Lane. Stay on main dirt road and follow the Hall Lake TH signs. After 1.2 miles you arrive at the parking area with TH sign and are basically in a clear cut.

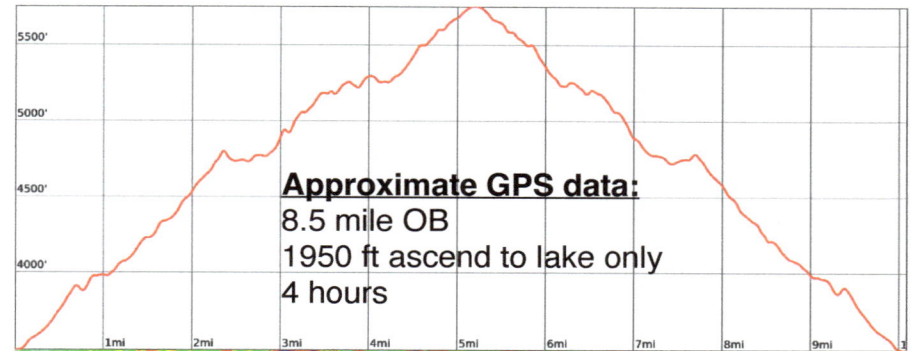

Approximate GPS data:
8.5 mile OB
1950 ft ascend to lake only
4 hours

Holland Falls

Overview: 3.3 mile OB. Starts at the East Holland TH near the bathrooms and signs at east end of parking lot. Stay right on trail #416 just after 0.1 miles. Trail #416 goes to Holland Falls.
- Trail in great shape and can be quite busy. Signs mark the trail.
- Decent shade on trail.
- Great views of Holland Lake and Mission Mountains across the Swan Valley.
- Good chance you may see or hear Loons on Holland Lake.

Getting to the TH: Take the Holland Lake Road south of Condon on Hwy 83. Go about 4 miles continuing by the campgrounds and day use picnic area. Road ends at large TH about half way down Holland Lake on the north side. TH has bathrooms.

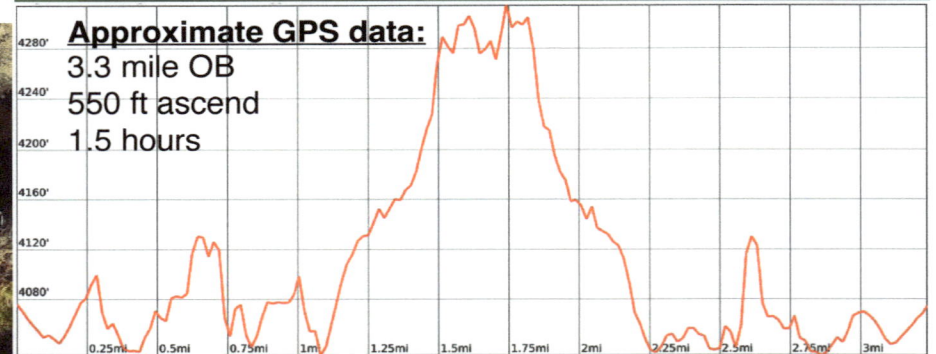

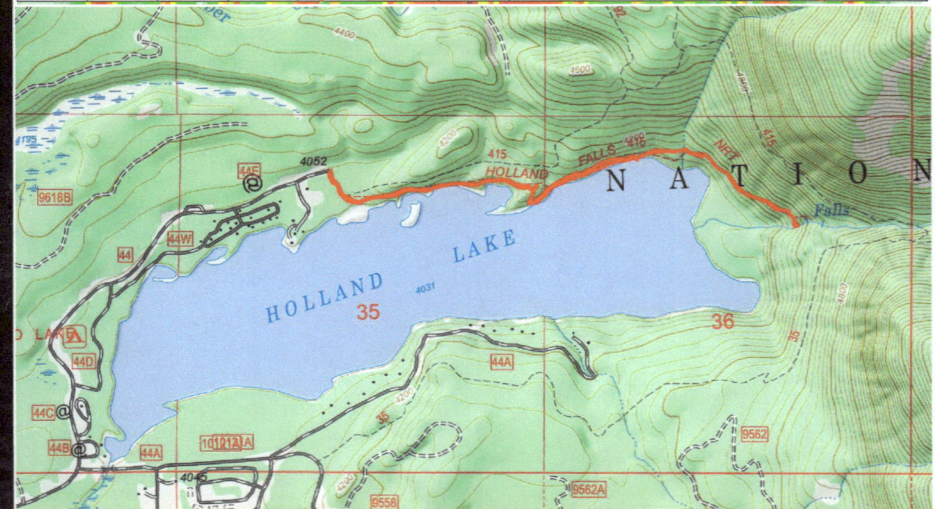

Approximate GPS data:
3.3 mile OB
550 ft ascend
1.5 hours

Holland Lookout

Overview: 11 mile OB. Starts at the East Holland TH near the bathrooms and signs at east end of parking lot. Stay left on trail at about 0.1 miles on Trail #415. Continue on Trail #415 for about a mile and stay right going by Trail #192. Shortly after, take left on Trail #42 for Holland LO. Over 4 miles of climbing and some switchbacks so start early while in the shade and cool. At about 4.1 miles, take left fork to go to the lookout.

- Awesome 360° views of Mission Mountains, Holland Lake, Lindbergh Lake, Swan Valley, Bob Marshall, Necklace and Sapphire Lakes.
- Climb is a good workout but views are worth it. Pick a fair weather day for the views.
- More exposure and views as you get higher.
- Trail in pretty good condition, but a little overgrown in spots. Had numerous down trees to cross in June. Snow sections can exist near the top into June and may need shoe spikes.
- Can be buggy especially lower.

Getting to the TH: Take the Holland Lake Road south of Condon on Hwy 83. Go about 4 miles continuing by the campgrounds and day use picnic area. Road ends at large TH about half way down Holland Lake on the north side. TH has bathrooms.

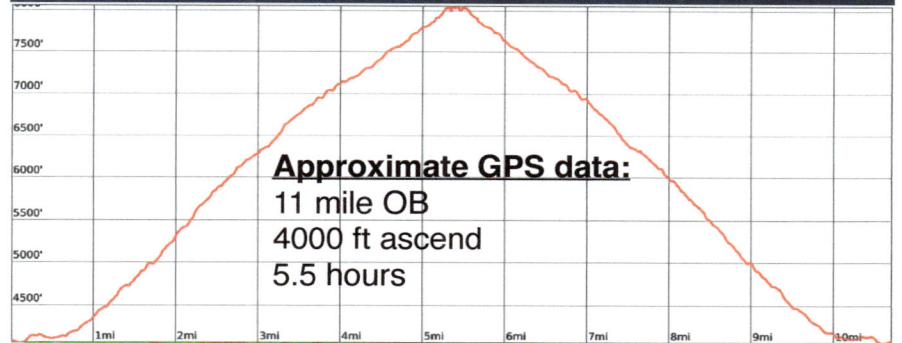

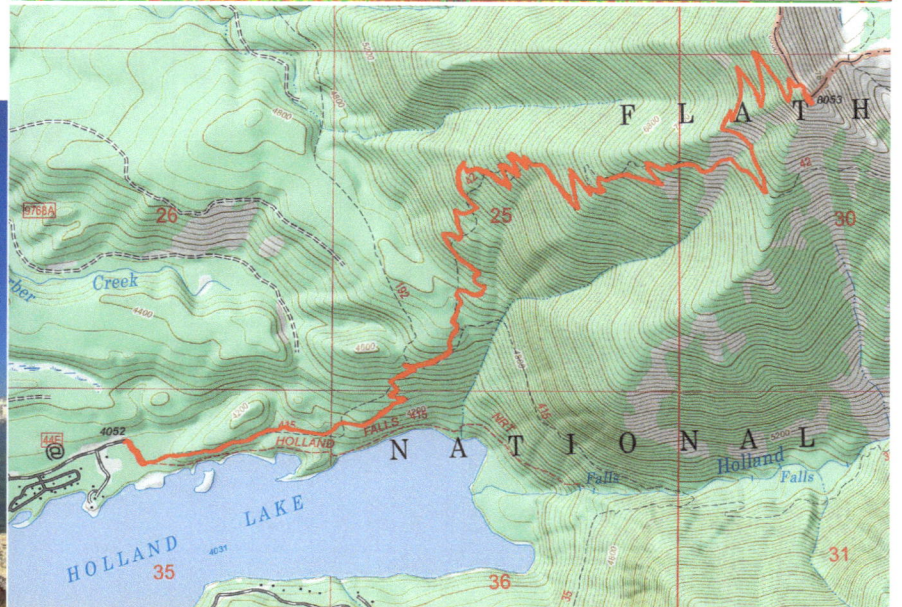

Approximate GPS data:
11 mile OB
4000 ft ascend
5.5 hours

Lower Rumble Creek Lake

Overview: 6.1 mile OB. Trail #192 starts climbing at reasonable grade before turning right (south) and leveling off. After crossing a series of 3 wooden bridges and at about 0.75 miles from the TH, take an unmarked left which starts climbing steeply. The next 1.2 miles climbs steeply for 2000 ft of elevation gain. This climb is a serious effort and only for those with some uphill fitness. After descending down a little and at about 2.2 miles from the TH you come to an open slope/slide with a steep washout area and you can see the trail on the far side of the slope...do not cross here the trail actually switchbacks and goes down through the trees and crosses below the steep washout... so take a right switchback and proceed steeply down the trail in the trees before it starts to cross the open slope. Poles help secure footing and from slipping. Cross the slope and proceed upward to the lower lake.

- **Caution:** As the TH sign says, the trail to Rumble Creek lakes is not an official Forest Service trail and not maintained. There is a trail and it is fairly easy to follow, but it climbs steeply and easy to slip on loose debris.
- I would not do this hike without trekking poles.
- Extremely steep grind. Trail is crude but can follow. Overgrown in spots. A number of fallen trees to traverse.
- Even with the aid of trekking poles descending, I managed to loose a toe nail. Didn't slide out though on the loose dirt and rocks.
- Scenic lake and view of Holland Peak.
- Beautiful in the fall with colors.
- Did not see anyone else on the trail or in the parking lot.

Getting to the TH: Take Hwy 83 south of Condon and just south of mile marker 41, and take left on Rumble Creek Rd #560 to East Foothill TH parking area with marked sign. Dirt road is roughly 3.7 miles to TH and you'll drive by the Cooney Lookout tower. No bathrooms at TH.

Approximate GPS data:
6.1 mile OB
2970 ft ascend
4.25 hours

Morrell Falls

Overview: 5.5 mile OB. Trail #30.
- Nice wide trail. Mostly flat and rolling with easy grades.
- Nice views of the falls and lake.
- I did this in the fall and didn't notice bugs, but I suspect there are many in the summer.
- Trail can be busy.

Getting to the TH: Head south on Hwy 83 towards Seeley Lake.   On the north end of Seeley Lake take a left on Morrell Creek Road 477 which has a marked green street sign. Take marked left for Morrell Falls TH on 4353. At 6.7 miles stay right on unmarked fork.   A forest service sign is a short ways after taking this fork.   At 7 miles stay left at fork for 4364 to Morrell Falls TH which is at 7.6 miles. TH has a bathroom.

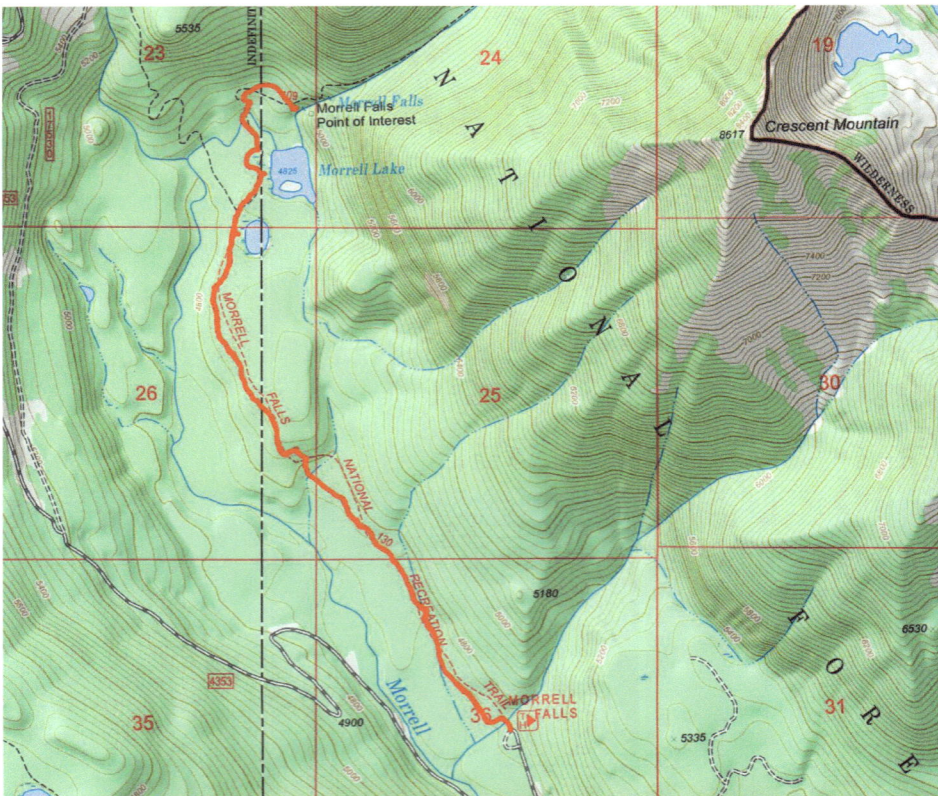

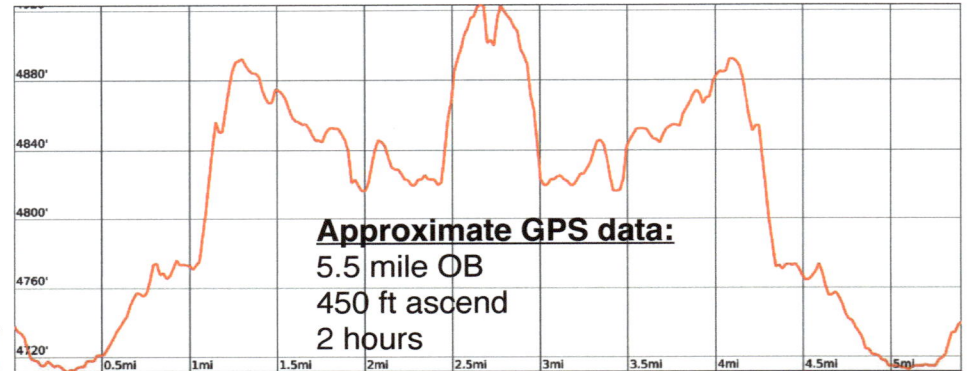

Approximate GPS data:
5.5 mile OB
450 ft ascend
2 hours

Necklace Lakes

Overview: 17 mile OB (shorter 15 mile OB option to the first couple of lakes). Starts at the East Holland TH near the bathrooms and signs at east end of parking lot. Stay left on trail at about 0.1 miles on Trail #415. Continue on Trail #415 for about a mile and stay right going by Trail #192. Shortly after, take left on Trail #42 for Holland LO. About 4 miles of climbing and some switchbacks so start early while in the shade and cool. Before getting to the top and going through a notch there is a left to go to the lookout, keep going straight which is now Trail #48 unless you want to go to the lookout. After going over the top and through the notch you descend a short ways with switchbacks and come to intersection with Trail #120. Take a left on Trail #120 to go to Necklace Lakes (right will go to Sapphire Lakes and Upper Holland Lake). There is a short climb over Necklace Pass before descending down towards the string of Necklace Lakes.

- Scenic lakes and views. Plenty of wildflowers.
- Trail in good shape and marked fairly well. Keep an eye out for the wood trail signs nailed to trees.
- The 4 mile section of climbing at the start is steady and a work out. Start early when cool. Recommend trekking poles.
- Take plenty of nutrition and drinks.
- Only saw a couple of backpackers the whole day.
- Keep an eye out for moose swimming and munching.

Getting to the TH: Take the Holland Lake Road south of Condon on Hwy 83. Go about 4 miles continuing by the campgrounds and day use picnic area. Road ends at large TH about half way down Holland Lake on the north side. TH has bathrooms.

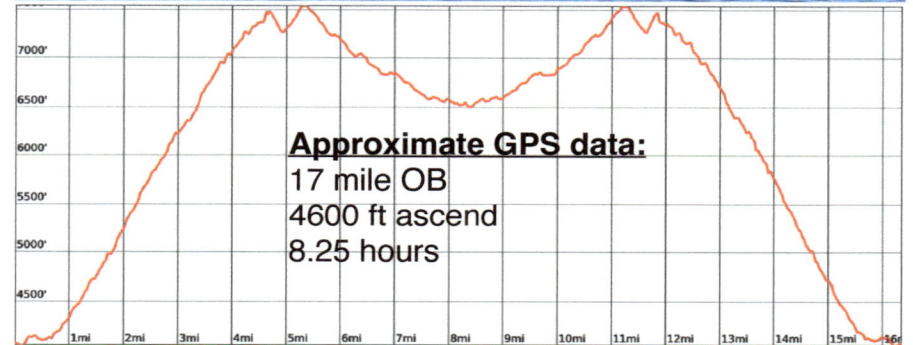

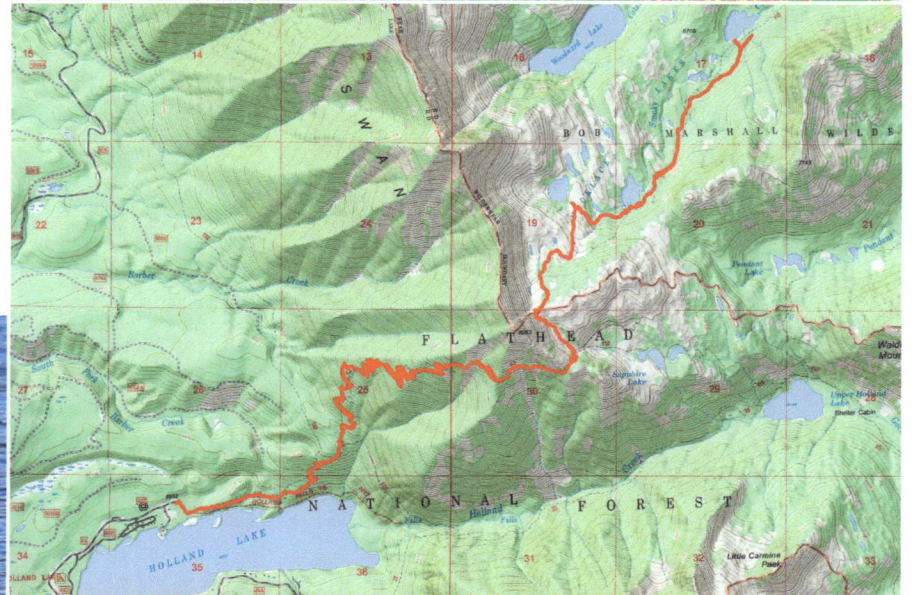

Approximate GPS data:
17 mile OB
4600 ft ascend
8.25 hours

Upper Holland - Sapphire Lake Loop

Overview: 13.4 mile clockwise loop hike. Starts at the East Holland TH near the bathrooms and signs at east end of parking lot. Stay left on trail at about 0.1 miles on Trail #415. Continue on Trail #415 for about a mile and stay right going by Trail #192. Shortly after, take left on Trail #42 for Holland LO. About 4 miles of climbing and some switchbacks so start early while in the shade and cool. Before getting to the top and going through a notch there is a left to go to the lookout, keep going straight which is now Trail #48 unless you want to go to the lookout. After going over the top and through the notch you descend a short ways with switchbacks and come to intersection with Trail #120. Take a right on Trail #120 to go to Sapphire Lakes and Upper Holland Lake. After going by Sapphire Lakes you descend down to Upper Holland Lake where you take a right at the intersection of Trail #35. Stay on Trail #35 and descend down from Upper Holland Lake. After a few miles of descending you come to a fork where you stay right on Trail #415 to return to East Holland TH and parking lot (a left goes on Trail #35 to Owl Creek TH).

- Doing loop counter clockwise has easier grade to Upper Holland Lake, but you have a warmer stiffer grade getting to Sapphire Lakes. Clockwise loop gets bulk of climbing done in shade and cooler if you leave early enough.
- Snow can persist longer above Sapphire Lakes. If unfamiliar with trails, clockwise may be easier to keep track of trail in snow spots looking from above as you descend.
- Trails in good shape and marked pretty well. Look for wood signs nailed to trees.
- If going counter clockwise and not familiar with the trails, it is easy to miss the left fork mid-way on Upper Holland Lake to Sapphire Lakes on Trail #120. The left fork is just before a rocky open slope. If you get to the end of the lake at Trail #110 to Pendant Pass you've gone too far.
- Take plenty of nutrition and drinks.
- Trekking poles helpful climbing and descending.

Getting to the TH: Take the Holland Lake Road south of Condon on Hwy 83. Go about 4 miles continuing by the campgrounds and day use picnic area. Road ends at large TH about half way down Holland Lake on the north side. TH has bathrooms.

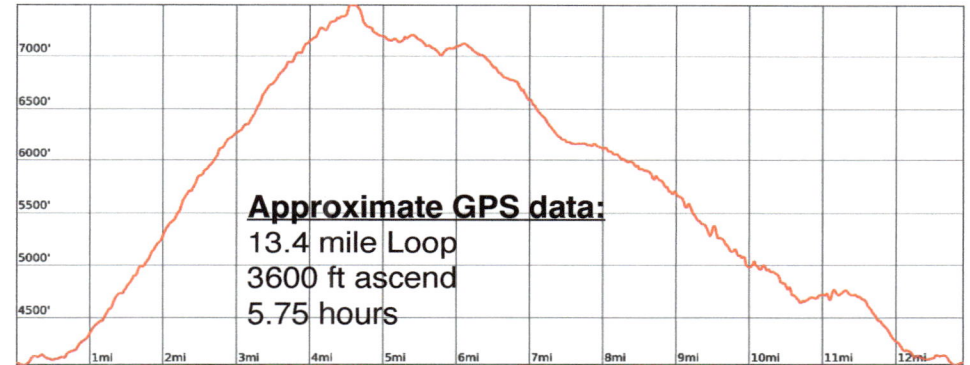

Approximate GPS data:
13.4 mile Loop
3600 ft ascend
5.75 hours

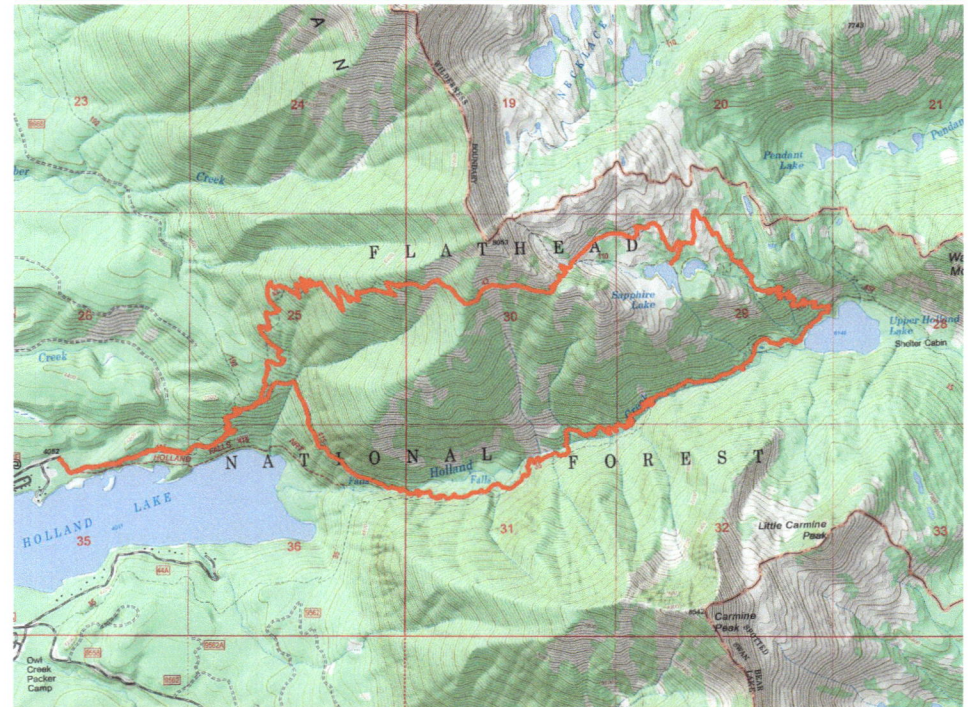

Upper Holland Lake

Overview: 11.3 mile OB. Starts at the East Holland TH near the bathrooms and signs at east end of parking lot. Stay left on trail at about 0.1 miles on Trail #415. Continue on Trail #415 for about a mile and stay right going by Trail #192. Shortly after, stay right going by Trail #42 for Holland LO. At about 2 miles you cross Holland Creek on a bridge and then shortly after stay left on Trail #35 at intersection to go to Upper Holland Lake (right goes back to Owl Creek TH).

- Nice views of Holland Lake and Mission Mountains.
- Trails in good shape and marked with signs.
- Grade fairly steady and not too bad.
- Trail has a lot of shade and can be buggy.

Getting to the TH: Take the Holland Lake Road south of Condon on Hwy 83. Go about 4 miles continuing by the campgrounds and day use picnic area. Road ends at large TH about half way down Holland Lake on the north side. TH has bathrooms.

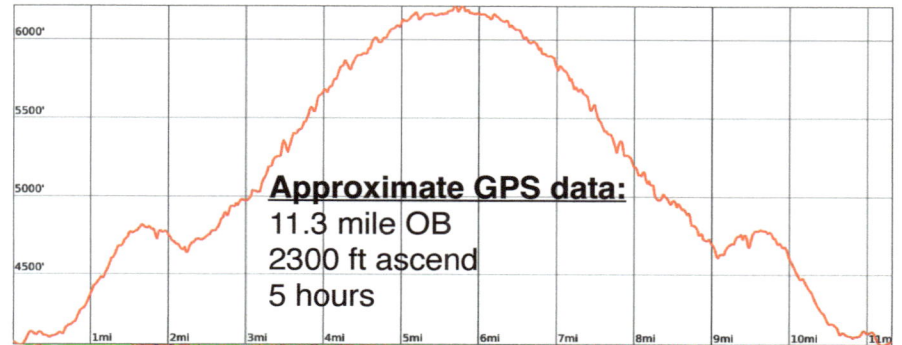

Approximate GPS data:
11.3 mile OB
2300 ft ascend
5 hours

Columbia Mountain

Overview: 12.25 mile OB. From the TH, trail #51 intersects with trail #7 at about 6 miles on the ridge at the top. Take a left on trail #7 for a short distance to a summit clearing for nice 360° views.

- Nice views of Flathead valley, Hungry Horse and peaks in Glacier National Park.
- Trails in good shape and trees with shade especially lower. Snow near top can persist into June.
- Grades are a workout but the views are worth it.
- You may see a black bear. I spotted one in early June.
- Can be busy first few miles, but may not see anyone after that.

Getting to the TH: Head east from Columbia Falls on Hwy 2 a short distance, after passing the House of Mystery as you turn along side the Flathead River, take a right on Berne Road. Berne Road is a short bumpy road to a large TH parking lot on the left.

Approximate GPS data:
12.25 mile OB
4900 ft ascend
6 hours

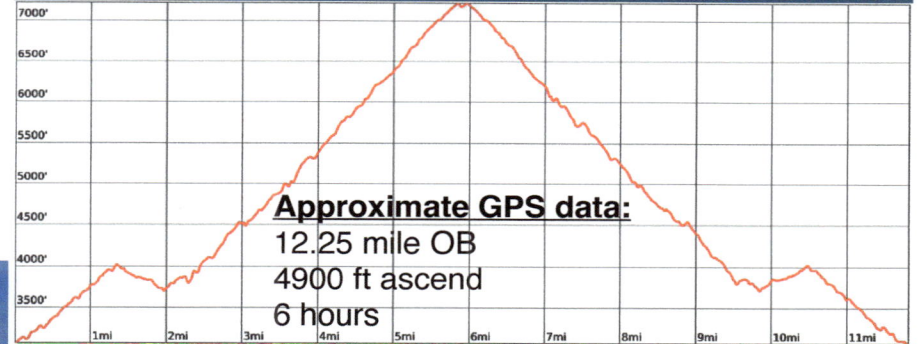

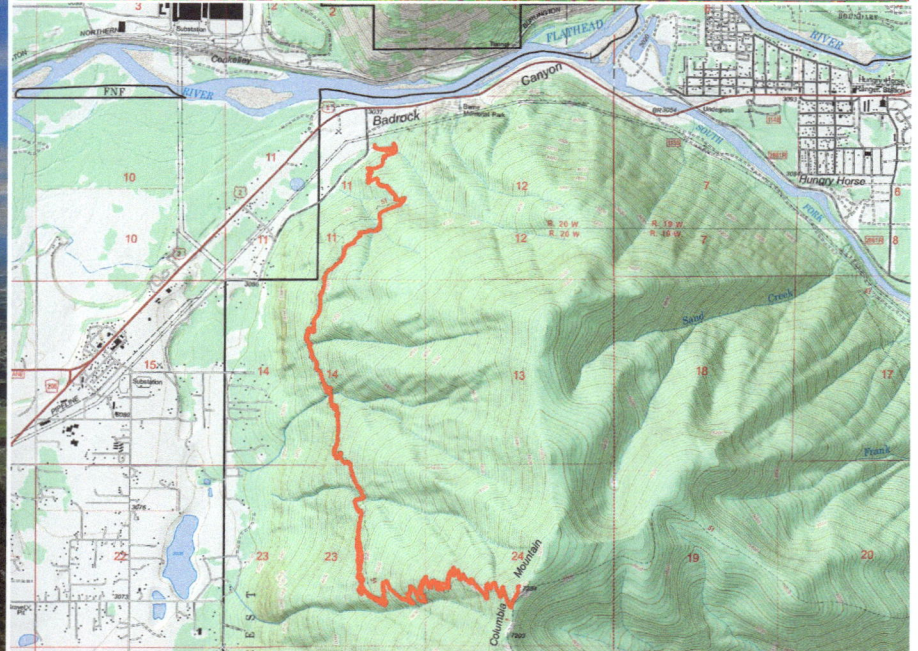

Firebrand Pass

Overview: 10.7 mile OB.   Trail is well marked. This hike is in Glacier National Park.

- Nice views at the pass and as you approach with more open exposure. Can be windy.
- Recommend fall for the colors and fewer bugs.
- Mosquitoes in July were very thick.
- There are some overgrown sections with thick brush between miles 2 to 3.5.
- Grades steady and not too bad, and get steeper as you approach the pass.
- Snow fields may exist into July. Check for trail status with the park.

Getting to the TH: Head east on Hwy 2 towards East Glacier. TH parking is on the left side of highway directly across from mile marker 203, and about 5 miles east of Marias Pass. The pullout drops below the highway on the left adjacent to the railroad so it is easy to miss. There is parallel parking for a number of cars. Cross the railroad and by an opening in a fence is a brown Glacier National Park trail sign. No bathrooms at TH, but Marias Pass rest stop about 5 miles back has restrooms.

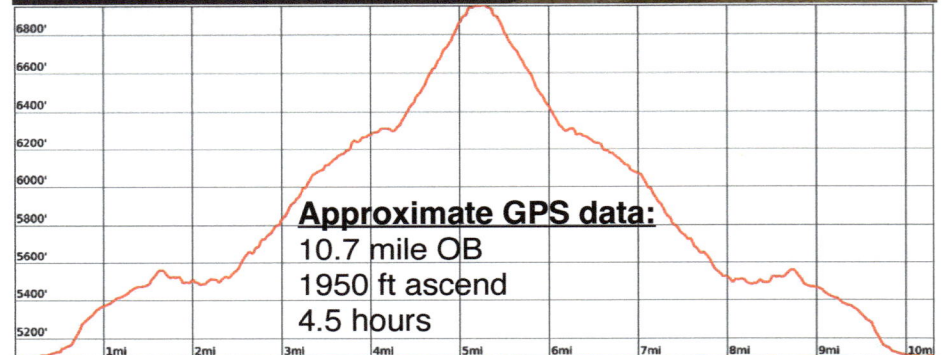

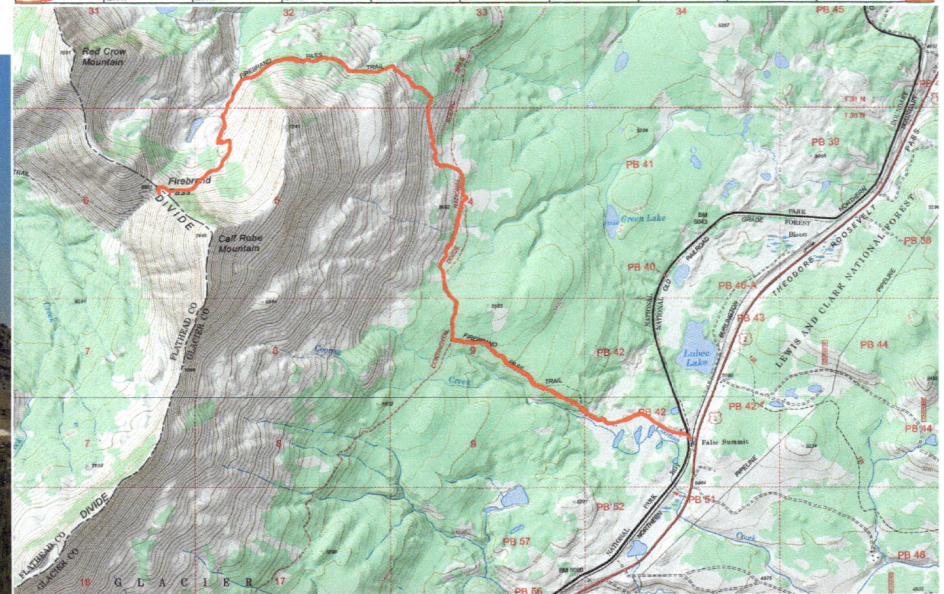

Approximate GPS data:
10.7 mile OB
1950 ft ascend
4.5 hours

Garry Lookout

Overview: 3.9 mile OB. Trail #499 is an old jeep trail. Lookout is gone but the top area is cleared for good views.

- Nice views of Mt. Saint Nicholas and Mt. Doody in Glacier National Park.
- Steady grade but pretty easy.
- Great winter hike option and popular for cross country skis and snow shoes. Trail is easy to follow and typically snow packed. Boots are fine unless there is fresh snow.

Getting to the TH: Head east on Hwy 2 past West Glacier and continue just past highway marker 168. There is a small pullout on the right for a few cars. Marked with sign for Trail #499.

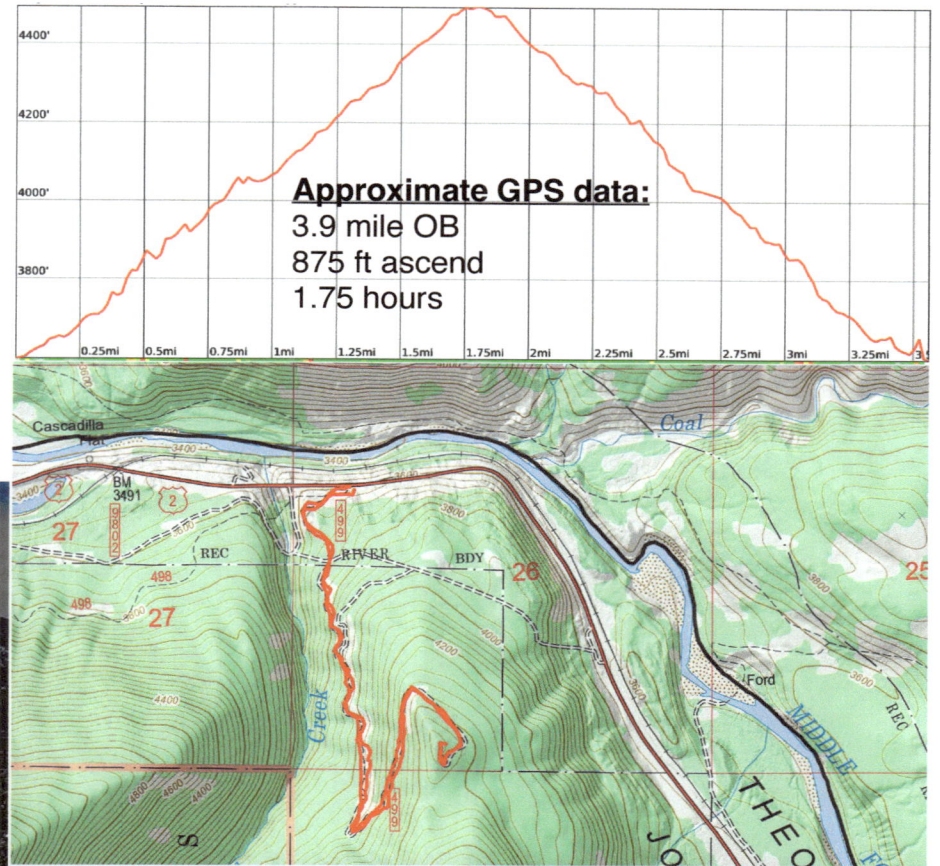

Approximate GPS data:
3.9 mile OB
875 ft ascend
1.75 hours

Loneman Lookout

Overview: 14.6 mile OB. This hike is for the adventurous souls and includes fording both the Middle Fork Flathead River and Nyack Creek, almost 4000 ft of climbing, long miles, some trail finding, and likely no human sightings. Locate the orange marker on the tree near the Hwy 2 overpass bridge, cross the railroad tracks and proceed to ford the Middle Fork with your fording shoes on (2 sections with a little island). Look for orange markers across the river. Once on the other side of the river, change into your hiking shoes. Follow orange markers and signs of the trail and after a short distance you come to a GNP trail mileage sign. Follow the trail past the old NPS cabins to the South boundary trail sign and then proceed left towards the Nyack creek crossing. Ford the Nyack creek with your fording shoes. Soon after you come to the Nyack creek trail sign and stay left at this intersection. About 0.1 miles from the Nyack creek trail sign is an unmarked fork, stay right for Loneman Lookout. After another 0.5 miles you come to another fork, this time with a GNP sign for Loneman Lookout and you stay right and begin climbing. About 5.4 miles from this sign to the LO.

- **CAUTION!!!** Fording the Middle Fork Flathead River can be dangerous especially early in the season with high water and strong current. Check with GNP Rangers if you have questions about the current fording conditions and TH details. If in doubt, don't cross.
- Recommend end of August or early fall to ford Middle Fork Flathead river with less water depth and current. Fall has fewer bugs and more colors.
- My crossing in early September was knee deep fording.
- **RECOMMEND** trekking poles to aid in crossings and staying up right, and also good water shoes for fording (not flip flops) with heal secured and some traction/foot protection. You also have to ford Nyack Creek which was slightly over knee deep in spots. I strapped my water shoes on the outside of my pack (you could probably find a hiding spot after fording the Nyack Creek). When fording, **unbuckle** your pack waist belt and chest strap so it is easier to exit the pack if you fall in.

- Thick overgrown brush along the trail in the early miles. Poles helped to push back the brush in some sections.
- Grades climbing are steady, not brutal, but still a workout.
- Trail is more exposed as you climb higher up the slope.
- Finally you are rewarded with nice views from the lookout and you have a nice view of Harrison Lake on the approach.

Getting to the TH: Head east on Hwy 2 from West Glacier and pull into the left hand side pullout directly across the road from the Skiumah creek TH sign. The pullout has a short narrow dirt road that descends down towards the railroad tracks. Park at the bottom in the grass. Proceed along the railroad tracks towards the Hwy 2 overpass going over the railroad tracks. As you approach the overpass, look across the tracks for an orange marker on a tree…this is where the adventure begins.

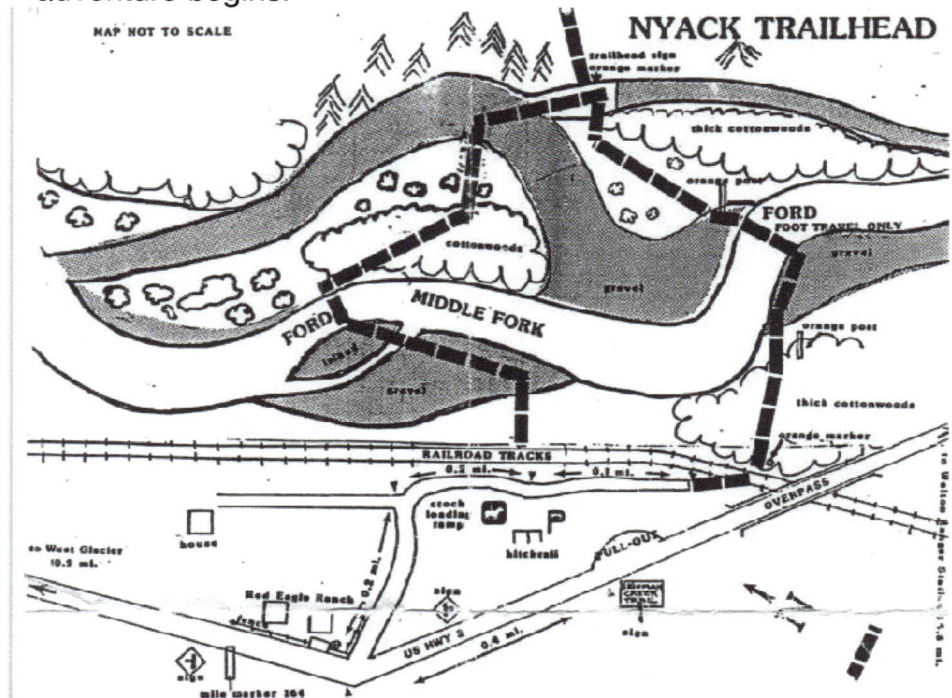

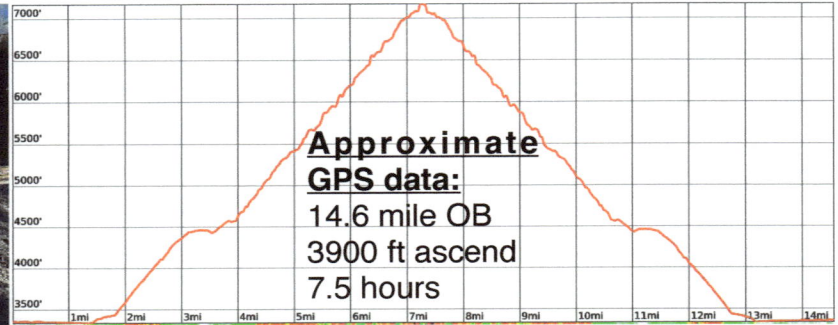

**Approximate
GPS data:**
14.6 mile OB
3900 ft ascend
7.5 hours

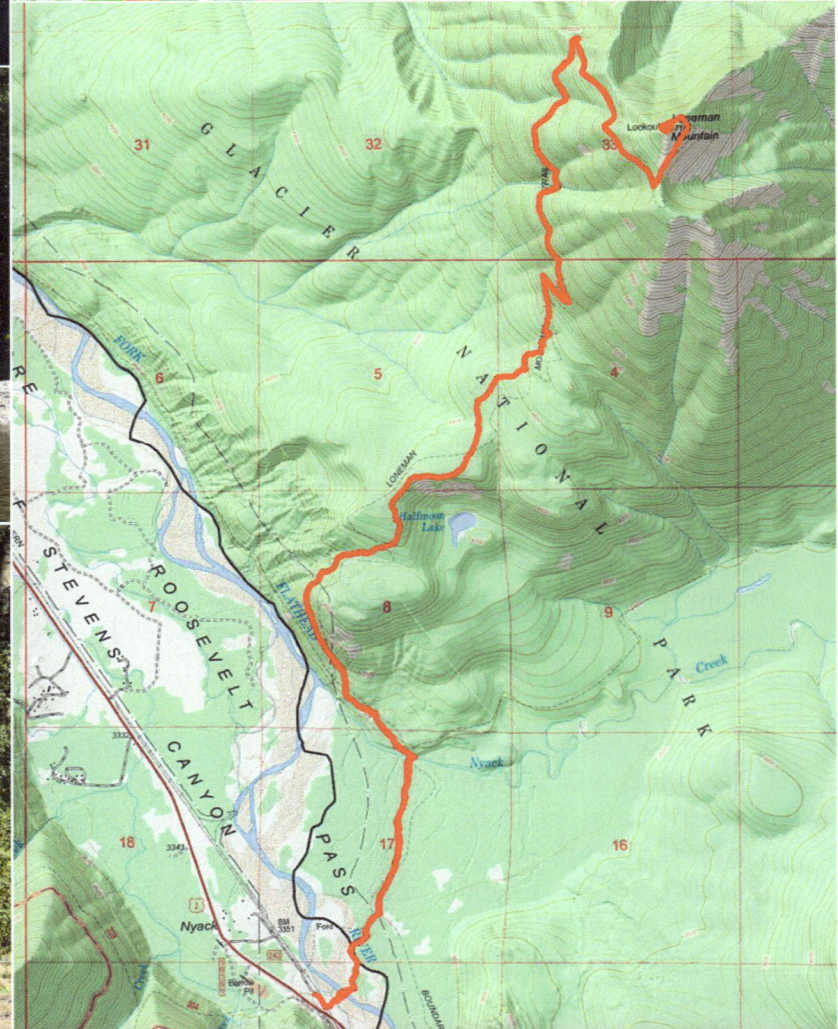

Marion Lake

Overview: 5.8 mile OB, shorter option is 4.5 mile RT to foot of lake. Trail #150.
- Trail is a little steep but not that long.
- Plenty of shade on trail.
- Can be buggy.
- A little overgrown in spots and more so if you proceed along the lake.
- Good hike if you don't want to see many people.

Getting to the TH: Near Essex off Hwy 2. Take Dickey Creek Road 1639 between mile markers 178 and 179. Cross the rail road tracks and then take immediate left on dirt road 1640. Go 2.4 miles and just before the road narrowing sign for Marion Creek Culvert there are several wide pullouts for parking. Back about 75 yards from the culvert is the trail heading up the hill and marked with a sign for Marion Lake.

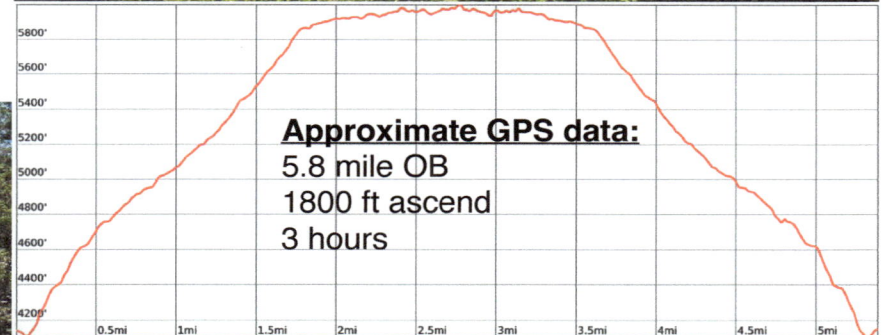

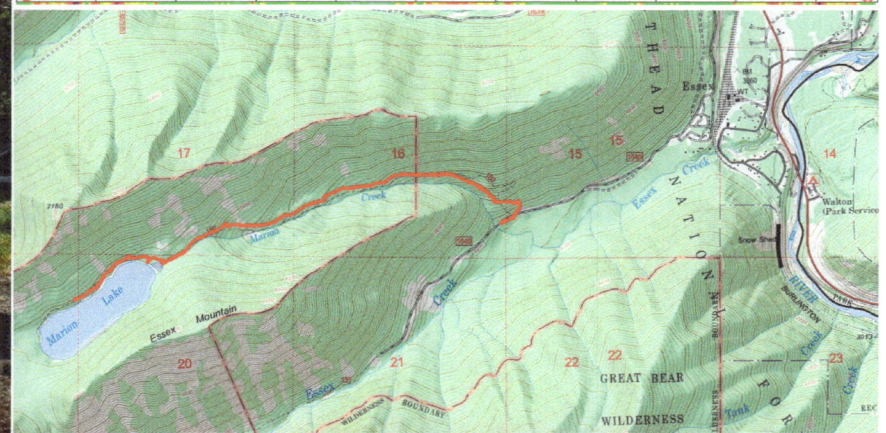

Approximate GPS data:
5.8 mile OB
1800 ft ascend
3 hours

Ousel Peak

Overview: 7.6 mile OB. Trail #331. This is a steep grade with rewarding views on the top. Recommend having some uphill fitness before attempting this hike.

- Trail is fairly steady, steep and a workout. 360° views on top are worth the effort. Views into southern Glacier National Park.
- Trekking poles help going up and down.
- Trail is in good shape and not technical, but gains about 1000 ft per mile.
- Plenty of shade on this trail.
- Recommend starting early before the day heats up.
- Pack plenty of drinks.
- Snow near top may persist into June but still doable.

Getting to the TH: Continue east on Hwy 2 from West Glacier for about 6 miles. On the right is a brown trail sign marking the trail going up the slope from Hwy 2. Just past the trail on the left side is a pullout for parking. You have to cross Hwy 2 to start the trail so be careful.

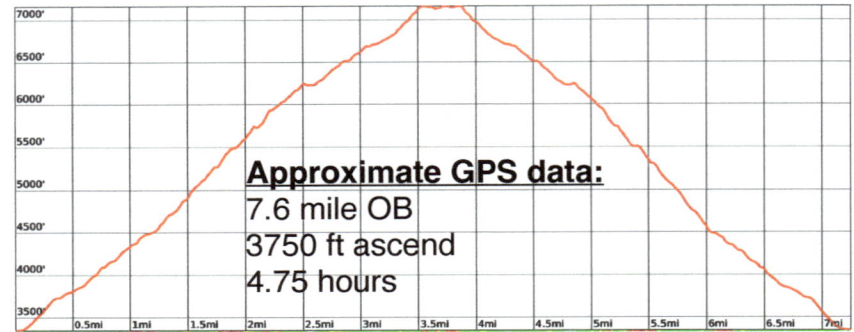

Approximate GPS data:
7.6 mile OB
3750 ft ascend
4.75 hours

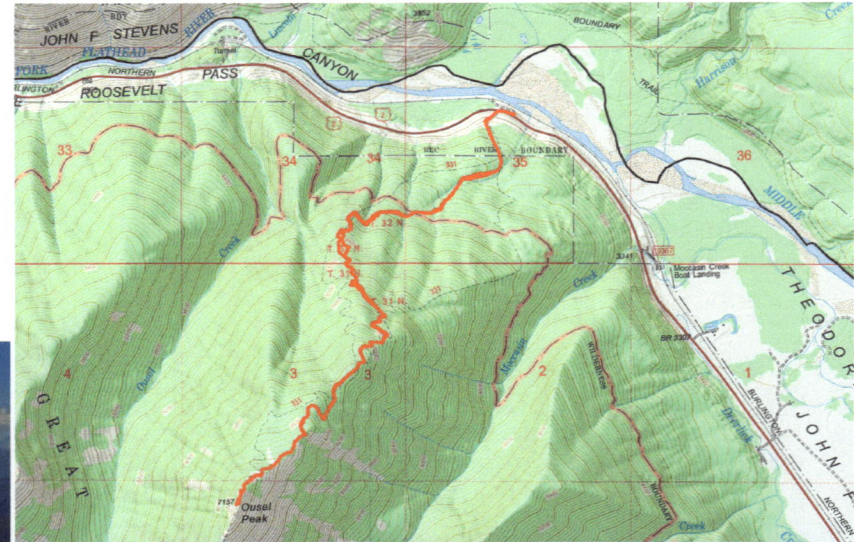

Scalplock Lookout

Overview: 9.5 mile OB. Trail is well marked. This hike is in Glacier National Park.

- Awesome views from LO including Mt Saint Nicholas.
- Nice hike and trail.
- Grades are not bad, with a few steeper switchbacks.
- Plenty of shade and more open as you get closer to the LO.
- Snow may exist near top into June.
- Not a busy trail and may not see anyone.

Getting to the TH: Head east on Hwy 2 past Essex and mile marker 180, cross the Middle Fork on Hwy 2 and take immediate left to Walton Ranger Station. Continue past the Ranger Station a short distance to picnic area and TH parking. Not too many parking spots, but I've never seen more than 3-4 cars here. Bathrooms at the trail head.

Approximate GPS data:
9.5 mile OB
3250 ft ascend
4 hours

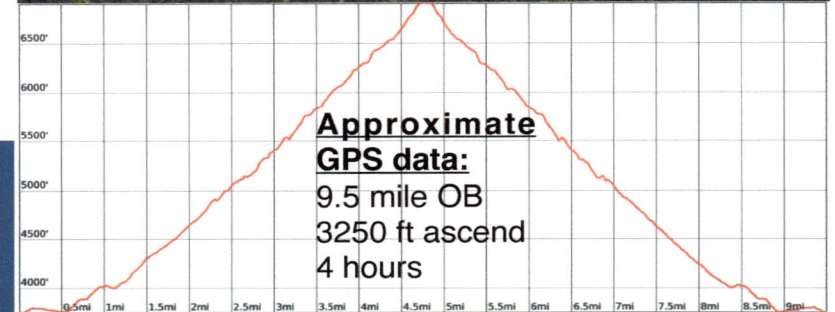

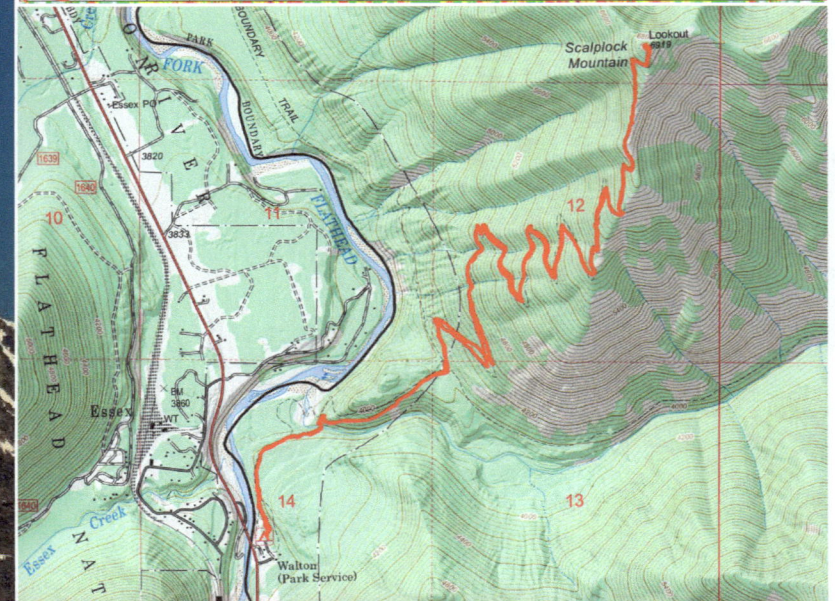

Skiumah Lake

Overview: 3.9 mile OB. Skiumah Creek Trail #204.

- A bit of climbing but grades not too bad.
- Plenty of shade.
- Buggy.
- For winter hike, park in plowed pullout opposite TH sign on Hwy 2 and hike a short distance along access road to the TH. Initial climbing traverses a steep slope so if packed snow and icy I strongly recommend quality shoe spikes, poles and/or snow shoes.

Getting to the TH: Head east on Hwy 2 from West Glacier about 8 miles. Look for Skiumah Creek Trail sign on right. Take short dirt road to TH and can be overgrown. The road circles back to Hwy 2.

Approximate GPS data:
3.9 mile OB
1125 ft ascend
2 hours

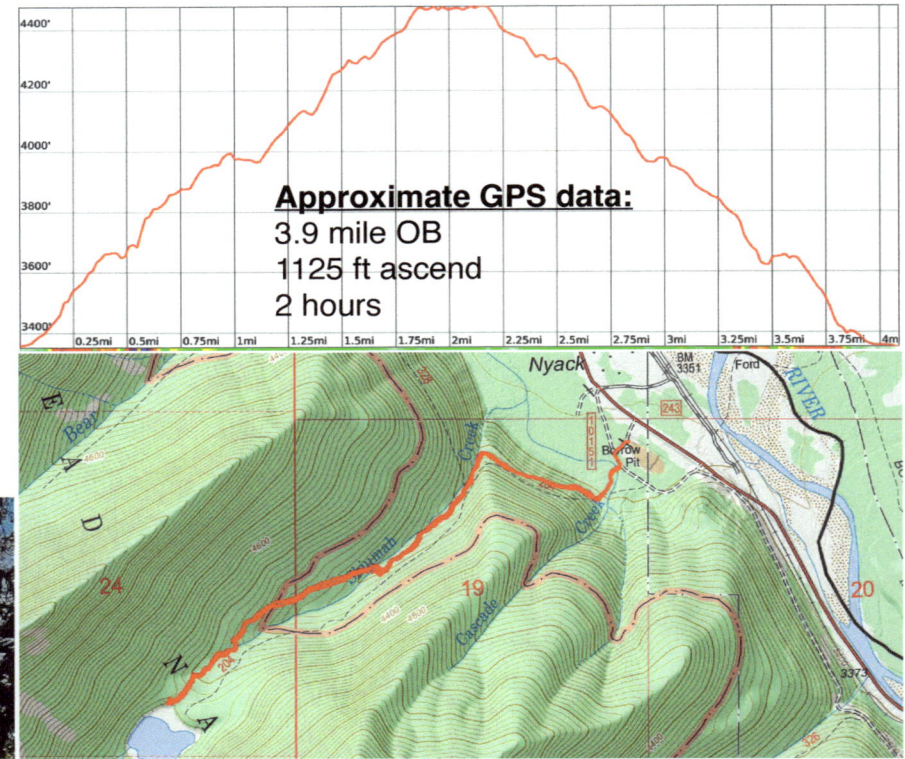

Stanton Lake

Overview: 4.9 mile OB includes hiking to the far end of lake. 2.6 mile OB to foot of lake. Stanton Lake Trail #146.

- Nice views from far end of the lake looking towards Glacier National Park.
- Most of the hardest climbing occurs right from the TH but fairly short.
- Plenty of shade.
- Buggy.
- Trail in good shape and can be busy.
- Popular winter hike option. The railroad plows the lot on the other side of Hwy 2 as a place to park your car.

Getting to the TH: Head east on Hwy 2 from West Glacier. Just before mile marker 170 and past Stanton Creek and brown trail head sign take a right into large gravel parking lot right off Hwy 2.

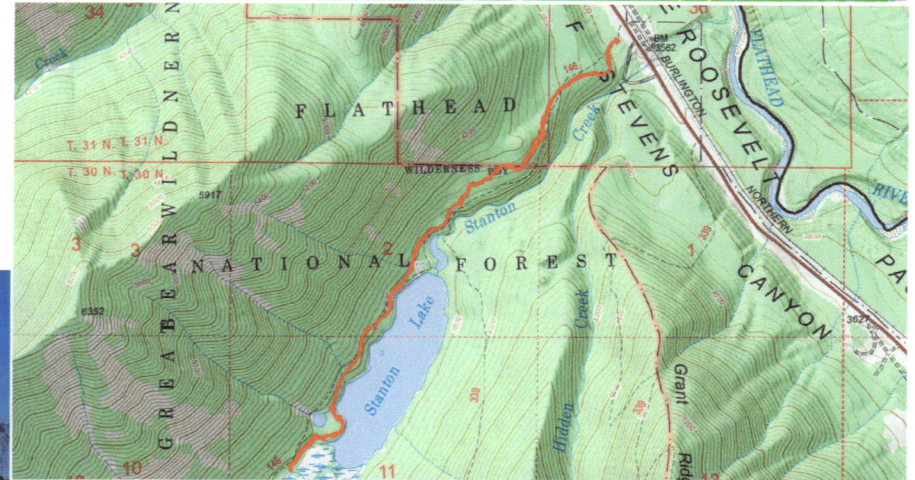

Approximate GPS data:
4.9 mile OB
675 ft ascend
2.5 hours

Additional Hikes

Danny On Trail

Overview: 8.9 mile OB. Danny On Trail.
- Trail in great shape and marked well.
- Some shade in sections.
- Grade is not too bad.
- Nice views.
- Nice close hike option if in Whitefish.
- Recommend fall for the colors.

Getting to the TH: From the city of Whitefish, follow signs to Whitefish Mountain Ski Resort. TH is marked and near chair lift #2 by Hellroaring Saloon building.

Approximate GPS data:
8.9 mile OB
2000 ft ascend
4 hours

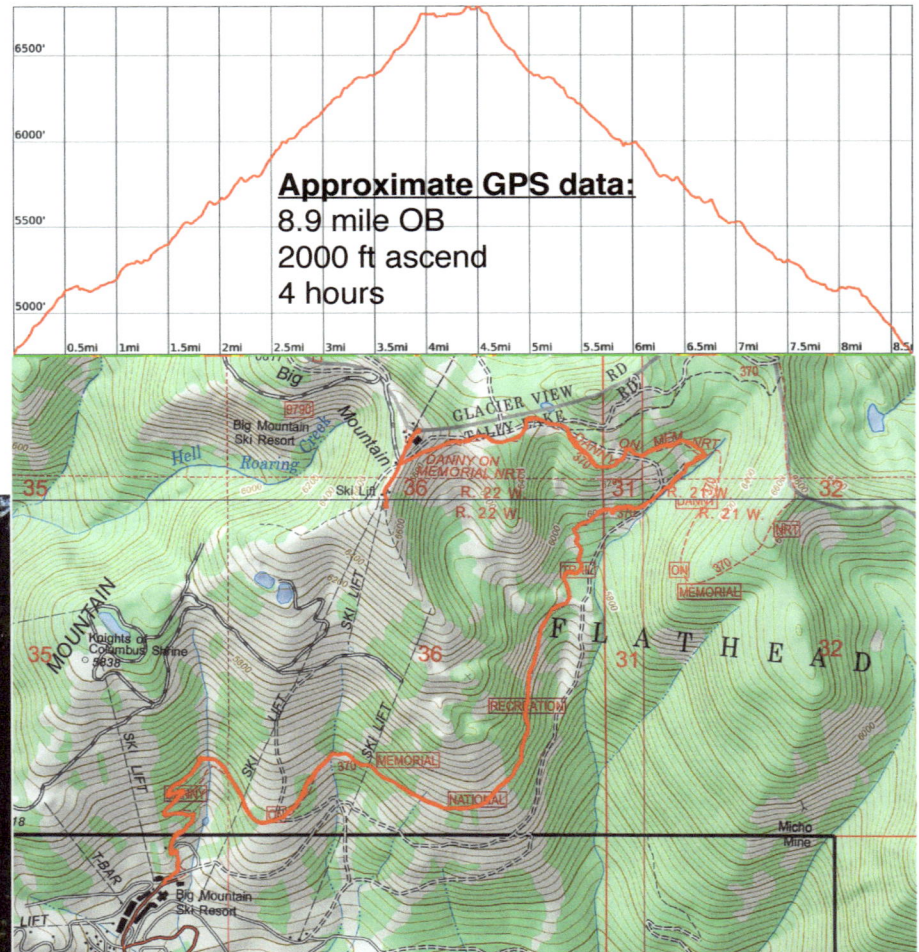

Lone Pine State Park

Overview: Numerous loop options all approximately 3 miles. Nice hiking year round near Kalispell. Loops described start from bottom at Valley View TH.
- Nice views of Flathead Valley and Swan Range.
- Trails in great shape. Winter can get icy and spikes needed.
- Well marked trails.
- Decent shade.
- Parking at both top and bottom.

Lone Pine trail up and Cliff trail down Loop:
- Proceed on the Valley View trail uphill until marked intersection with Cliff trail and take right on Cliff trail back down hill towards bottom and intersection with Lone Pine Trail.
- At marked wide Lone Pine Trail intersection take a left for loop and it will proceed flat for awhile before starting uphill.
- Continue uphill on wider Lone Pine trail to almost the top.
- At about 1.9 miles, near top on Lone Pine trail there will be a single track trail on the left heading uphill to the view points…take the left.
- Proceed past the views and then down to cross the bridge. Once crossing the bridge take 2 immediate rights and proceed downhill on the Cliff trail towards the bottom on single track.
- At marked trail intersection with Valley View Trail, take a right on this trail back to the parking lot.

Raptor Rest loop:
- Start on Valley View trail for about 50 yards to a left marked fork for Raptor Rest Trail. Take Left.
- Stay left on 4 branches to do outer most loop and will include sections of the Bearly There Trail and Cliff Trails near the top. On the Cliff Trail near the top proceed under the bridge and continue around covered picnic tables to Lone Pine Trail and take a right on this wide trail.
- Continue downhill on the wide Lone Pine Trail to the bottom.

- Along the bottom of Lone Pine trail you will come to a marked right hand uphill turn for the Cliff trail. Take it.
- Short uphill on Cliff trail to marked left hand turn for Valley View trail back to the parking lot.

Getting to the TH: Heading south on Alternate US 93 on the west side of Kalispell, take the Foys Lake exit and take right exit from round about on Valley View Drive. Drive short distance past some homes and a couple of 90 degree corners before coming to marked right hand turn for Lone Pine State Park. Decent parking lot just up the hill.

Approximate GPS data: Variety ~3 mile loops, 750 ft ascend, 1 hour

Lone Pine up,
Cliff down Loop

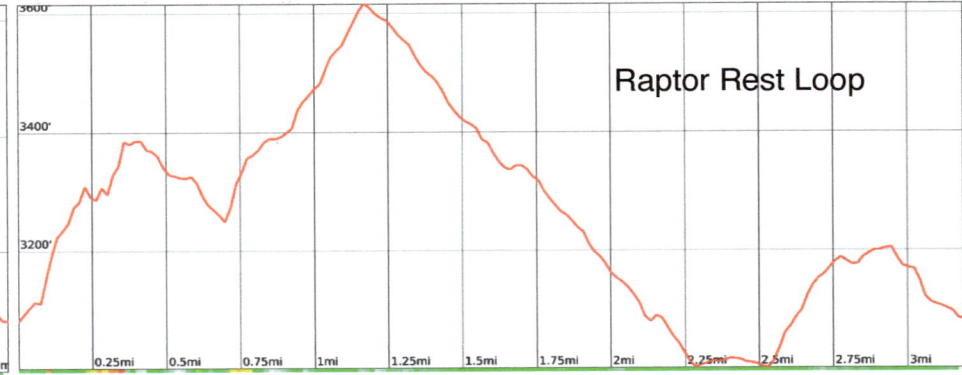

Raptor Rest Loop

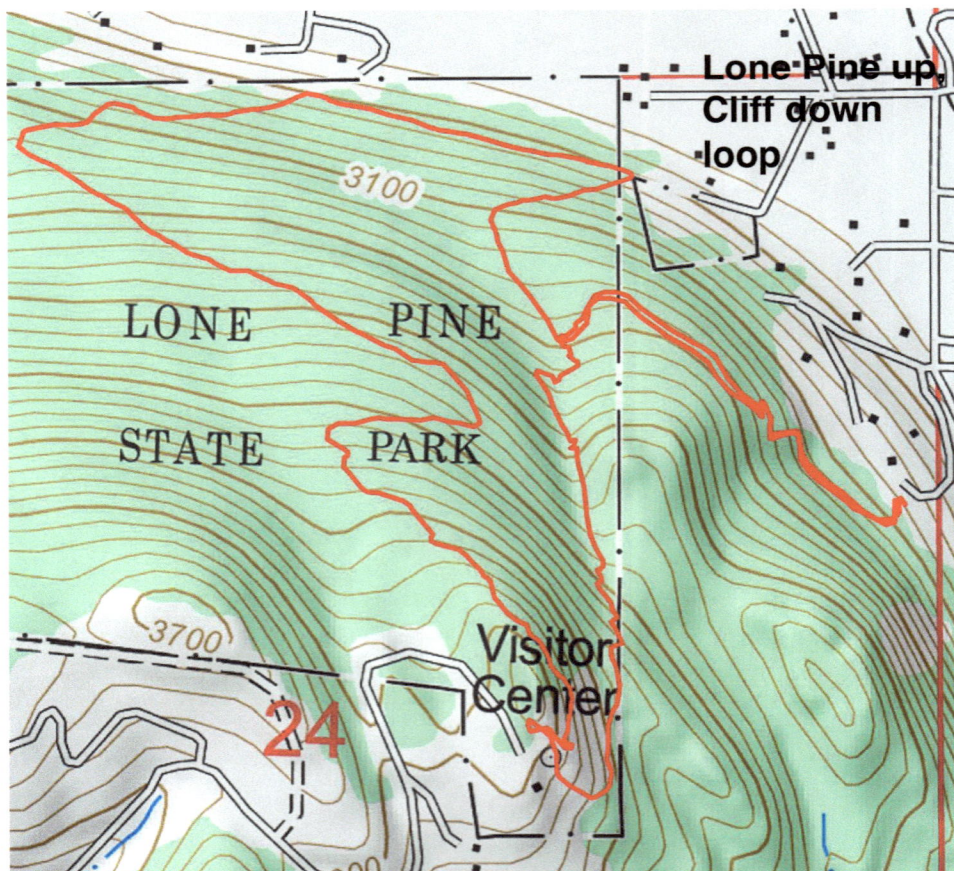

**Lone Pine up,
Cliff down
loop**

LONE   PINE

STATE   PARK

3100

Visitor
Center

3700

24

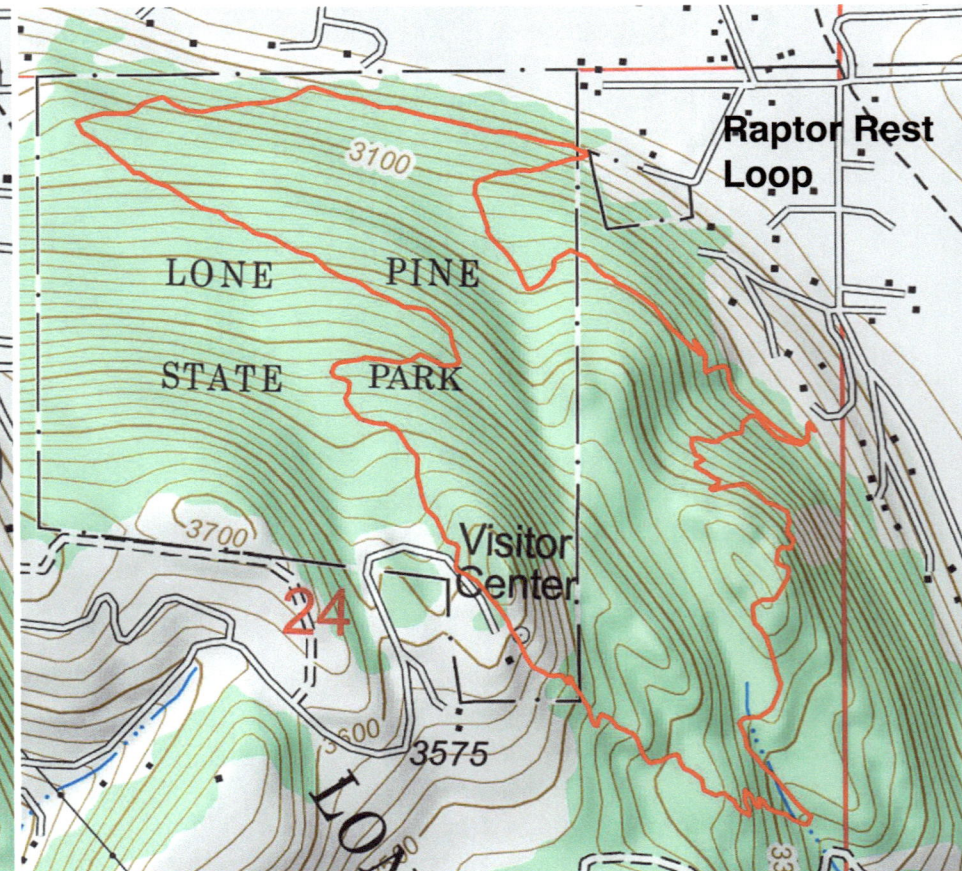

**Raptor Rest
Loop**

LONE   PINE

STATE   PARK

3100

Visitor
Center

3700

24

3575

Smith Lake via Smith Creek Loop

Overview: 5.5 mile OB/loop. Trail is well marked.
- Nice views of the lake.
- Nice trail, wide, smooth and mostly flat to rolling. Not too much climbing and grades pretty easy.
- Trail is mixed forest with shade, and open clear cut fields.
- Trail is shared with mountain bikes.
- Trail can get a little busy.

Getting to the TH: From the town of Whitefish, drive towards the end of Whitefish Lake on E. Lakeshore Drive and look for Swift Creek TH pullout on the right. Short dirt road to the TH. Plenty of parking, map and info, bathroom on the right end past TH signage.

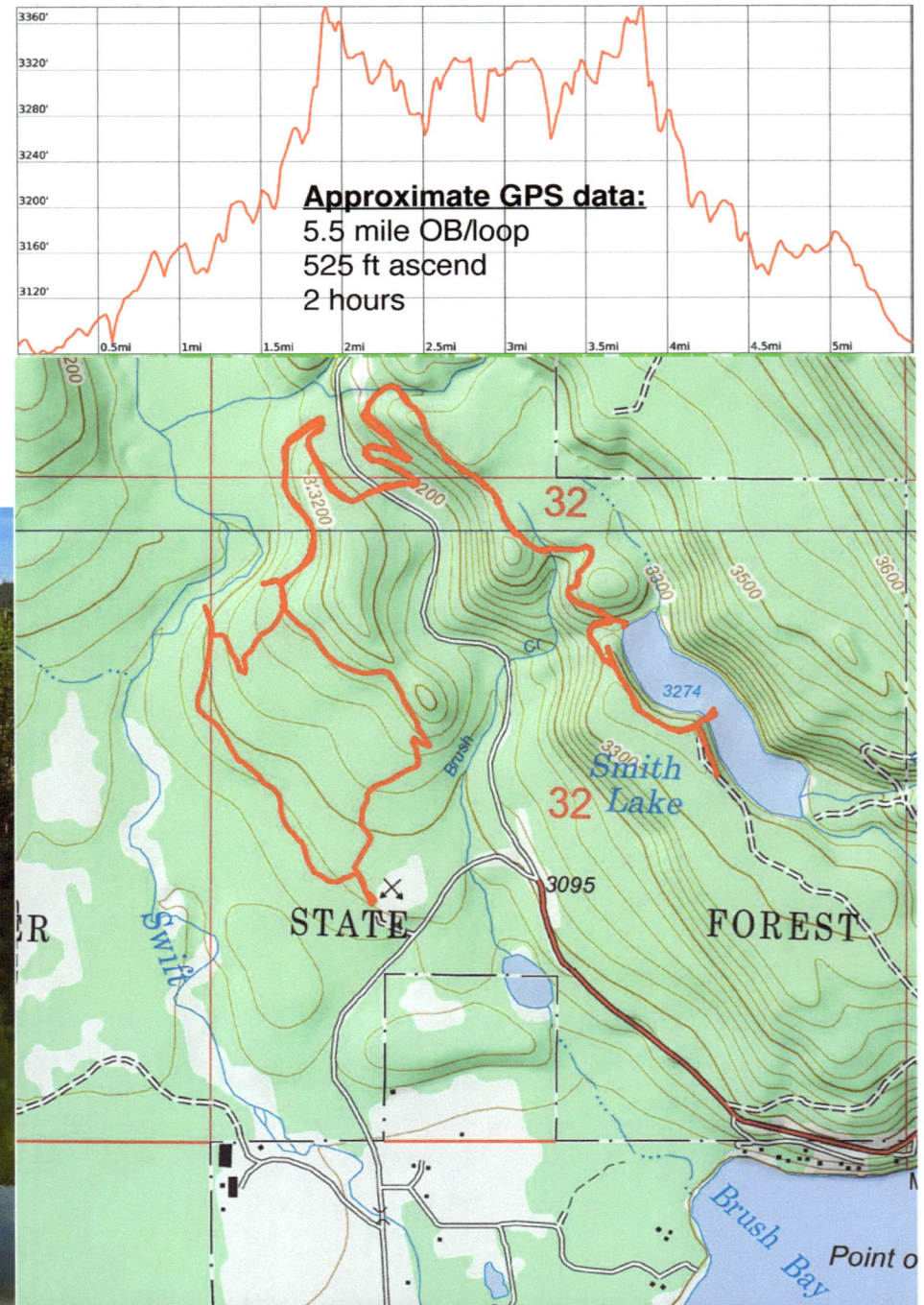

Approximate GPS data:
5.5 mile OB/loop
525 ft ascend
2 hours

Swan River Nature Trail

Overview: 4.5 mile OB. Basically flat unless you park in downtown Bigfork and hike up the hill to the TH.
- Flat hike along Swan River.
- Nice hike option all year around. Spikes can help if icy.
- Dam is located at about the half way point with rapids below it.
- Bald Eagles can sometimes be spotted soaring or perched in the trees along side the river.

Getting to the TH: Some parking at TH in Bigfork. Take Grand Drive up the hill from downtown to TH. I normally parallel park in downtown Bigfork on Grand Drive and walk up the hill. Parking also at other end of the trail just across the Swan River bridge heading towards Ferndale a few miles on Hwy 209. The large parking lot at the Ferndale end of the trail has a bathroom. There is also a bathroom at about the half way point by the Dam.

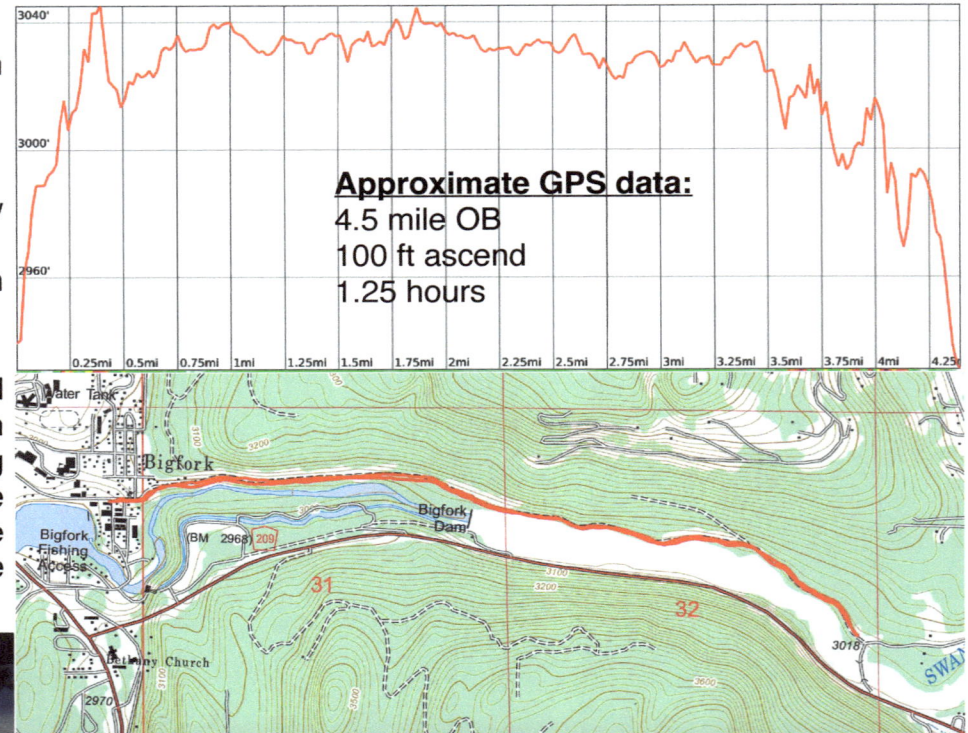

Approximate GPS data:
4.5 mile OB
100 ft ascend
1.25 hours

www.ingramcontent.com/pod-product-compliance
Lightning Source LLC
Chambersburg PA
CBHW041550030426

42335CB00004B/177